five pounds of fibroids: a memoir

Rose Marie Johnson

Rose Marie Johnson Publishing
ISBN-13: 978-0578416632
ISBN-10: 0578416638

Cover design by Elena Kovach
instagram.com/photographer_elenakovach

Cover and author photographs by Rose Marie Johnson
fivepoundsoffibroids.com

This book is sold with the understanding that the author is neither engaged in recommending, suggesting nor interpreting medical information. Expert medical advice pertaining to evaluation of symptoms and diagnosis of uterine fibroid tumors should be sought from competent medical professionals.

Due to the dynamic nature of the Internet, website addresses or links contained in this book may have changed since publication and may no longer be valid.

Printed in the U.S.A.

In loving memory of my magnificent mother,
Mary Elizabeth Johnson, a Queen, Saint, and Teacher
of love, compassion, and courage
– the epitome of motherhood.

To my fantastic father,
James Marion Johnson, a King, Protector, and Teacher
of love, compassion, and courage
– the epitome of fatherhood.

Contents

Acknowledgments

Handshakes, hugs, and hefty gift baskets fall short in expressing my gratitude to the most honest, compassionate, patient-centric medical professionals, Shelley Susman, M.D., OB/GYN and Scott M. Eisenkop, M.D., Gynecological Oncology, OB/GYN. I am also indebted to Maurice Dicterow, M.D., April D'Aqurmao, and affable operating room team, specialists, nurses, and staff at Sherman Oaks Hospital.

Tremendous thanks to my extraordinary editor, Dr. Susan Sosoo, for her expertise, honesty, and tireless efforts in polishing the manuscript. And, I thank my fantastic family and wonderful relatives, especially Felicia Bray, Christine Glasgow, and Sharon Bray, for their undying love and prayers.

Friends are hard to come by and I am grateful to have many of the greatest. Special thanks to Tony Robinson, an amazing friend who demonstrated the epitome of kindness during the most turbulent period of my life. Deepest thanks to Bob Dempsey and Lance Fessler for sheltering me amid several storms with bigheartedness and generosity. And, wholeheartedly, I thank Novak Kneeland, Elena Kovach, Yuri Medina, Jordan Alatorre, GiGi Green, Lauri Rank, Tceci Galvan, Marsha Miller, Nicholas Tana, Brandon Milligan, Rebecca Buenrostro, Emilio Acevedo, Maria De Jesus Rodriquez, Karen Laws, Yizreel Vidrio, Peggy Matucci, Erika Manzagol, Hunter Wakatsuki, Sebastian "Sebas" Brily, Alicia Gatto, James Gleason, Ann Wolfe, the Martinez family, the Nunez family, Azmul and Mila Khan, Kris and Dalida Hairabedian, partners at Starbucks of Fullerton, North Hollywood and Sherman Oaks, California, and many other great friends for their unwavering love, support, and encouragement.

Last, but not least, I deeply thank my Bichon-Friese, Prince. Had it not been for him, I may not have made it off the kitchen floor and into the emergency room.

Author's Note

Standing in the doorway wearing required instructors' attire, a white oxford shirt and light-colored khakis, I greeted each student as they entered the classroom. There were roughly twelve that evening with backgrounds ranging from college students to CEOs. Since most attended word processing and database design classes I taught at the computer store, I sensed their excitement in taking a more creative one this time around.

Approximately ten minutes prior to starting the class, an eager student asked that I show her how to insert an image into a presentation she created on her own. Although I had planned to cover the topic toward the tail end of the four-hour session, her enthusiasm prompted me to assist.

As I leaned toward her monitor to explain the steps, pain which felt like fiery logs of flesh exploding inside my uterus struck. Radiating throughout my lower abdomen and back, I crouched onto her desk. Suddenly, blood began charging out of me at what felt like fire hydrant speed. Piercing through the sides of my panties and streaming down my legs, within seconds, bright red bloodstains saturated my khakis.

Startled by sounds of shuffling chairs and students dashing toward me, I lifted myself off the desk, hobbled down the aisle, and hid behind the instructor's podium. Sitting cross-legged on the stool, a student in her early 60s rushed over and whispered, *"What's wrong?"* Too flabbergasted to speak, I uncrossed my legs and pointed toward the seat of my pants. Straightaway, she announced I had *"fallen ill"* and ended the class.

Closing the door behind the last student, she placed her arm around my shoulder and asked if I had ever bled this heavily before. *"Heavy, yes, but never with balls of blood raging out of me."*, I said. *"You're expelling blood clots and may have fibroids, my dear. Let's get you to the restroom."*, she said.

Since neither she nor I had anything to cover my lower half, I resisted her attempts at raising me to my feet. The mere thought of customers and store personnel seeing me bloodied, terrified me. It was demoralizing enough my students likely caught glimpse of my bloody splendor moments ago. But, realizing my only options were to sit soaked until the store closed or have her escort me to the restroom, I finally stood.

As I turned to look at the light gray stool, I was dumbstruck. Not only was it drenched, droplets of blood had spattered onto the carpet beneath it. Compelled to clean up the horrendous mess knowing a class was scheduled the next morning, I clutched my crotch with my left hand to prevent ruining anything else. With my right hand, I ripped sheets out of a leftover training manual and began wiping blood off the stool. However, the onslaught of another surge forced me to stop.

Limping toward my reassuring student, she grasped onto my arm and opened the classroom door. Seeing how packed the store was, I pleaded, *"I can't go out there. They're going to see blood all over me."* Without response, she yanked me out the door with every bit of her strength. And, as we walked past droves of customers, I felt like the main character in the movie *Carrie*[1] with *"They're all gonna laugh at you."*, echoing to no end.

Standing guard outside, I entered the single-stall restroom. Without a change of pants, I didn't know where to begin. After

---

[1] *Carrie*, written by Stephen King, directed by Brian De Palma, United Artists, 1976.

removal, I placed them under cold running water. As I alternated between scrubbing and wringing for several minutes, a torrent of blood matter began gushing out of me so fast, I slammed my legs together and staggered to the toilet.

Petrified to tears, I sat wiggling my panties below my hips. Seeing the gore-soaked pad overflowing with heaps of coagulated blood that my student called *"blood clots"* made me so squeamish, I couldn't suppress my gasps. To circumvent spillage onto the floor, I pulled my panties upward and emptied what looked like a nest of bloody egg yolks into the toilet.

Vomiting at the sight of colonies of clots lodged in the bowl while tugging on the toilet paper roll, I heard what sounded like agitated knocking on the door. In speechless tremor, I stuffed a sanitary pad between my legs and stood pulling my bloodstained panties over my hips. Unwinding another bundle, I moved to the sink to wet it and began wiping smudges of blood off the toilet seat and traces of vomit off the floor — praying I wouldn't provoke another blood rush.

After hastily washing my hands, I stepped into my soggy pants and fastened them. As I opened the door, I expected a barrage of furious women ready to berate me for occupying the restroom for nearly fifteen minutes. Instead, I was met by my student who had knocked out of concern. Like an angel, she shielded me with her body as we walked through the jam-packed computer store and exited.

Introduction

Assaulted by menstrual cramps at age 14 and a string of premenstrual syndrome (PMS) symptoms by age 16, much of my adolescence was reduced to popping pain pills and lying in the fetal position. When ambushed by premenstrual dysphoric disorder (PMDD) in my mid-20s, I dreaded my periods altogether. And, just when my tolerance of menstruation-related issues had reached its peak, ferocious fiends called fibroids reared their ugly heads in my late 30s.

Growing inside me, undiagnosed, several years prior, my fibroid-infested uterus often brought forth humongous blood clots, violent abdominal pain, spine-twisting back pain, chronic constipation, frequent urination, abdominal bloating, chronic anemia, and a host of other symptoms.

Although life altering and ruinous, I kept my 15-year melee with fibroids a hush-hush out of fear, shame, and embarrassment. And, as a relatively private person, I never imagined sharing my insufferable battle against fibroids with the world. But, knowing this bamboozling condition affects 1 in 4 women of child bearing years in the United States[2] and countless women globally, it would have been criminal to keep my plight to myself. In fact, a study conducted in 2003 revealed, "*The estimated cumulative incidence of tumors by age 50 was >80% for black women and nearly 70% for white women.*"[3]

A long-standing recipient of this debilitating disorder, I know the challenges symptomatic fibroid sufferers face. I sympathize with women whose symptoms are so taxing that their quality of life, relationships, and careers are negatively affected. I can relate to those who are uncertain of steps to take after diagnosis and understand how frustrating continuous experimentation with traditional and alternative medicines and therapies can be.

Furthermore, I can identify with women who have undergone one or more fibroid removal or shrinkage procedures and are confounded when fibroids grow back larger and more

---

[2] Luckstein, K. "Exploring Treatment Options for Women with Fibroids." *Mayo Clinic*, 23 Apr. 2015, www.newsnetwork.mayoclinic.org/discussion/exploring-treatment-options-for-women-with-fibroids/.
[3] Baird, DD., Dunson, DB., et al. "High Cumulative Incidence of Uterine Leiomyoma in Black and White Women: Ultrasound Evidence." AJOG, Jan. 2003, Vol. 188, no. 1, pp. 100-107, doi.org/10.1067/mob.2003.99, Abstract.

symptomatic than before. And, I also understand why some tolerate horrendous symptoms for many years, hoping fibroids will either shrink or disappear at menopause.

As I prayed for a fibroid-zapping miracle, I searched high and low for books written by women stricken with symptomatic fibroids. Other than Carla Dionne's *Sex, Lies, and the Truth about Uterine Fibroids*, Monique R. Brown's *It's A Sistah Thing: A Guide to Understanding and Dealing with Fibroids for Black Women*, and Johanna Skilling's *Fibroids: The Complete Guide to Taking Charge of Your Physical, Emotional, and Sexual Well-Being,* such books were and still are few and far between.

I also engrossed myself in reading several self-help and medical books including *Uterine Fibroids: The Complete Guide* by Elizabeth A. Stewart, M.D., *Natural Treatment of Fibroid Tumors and Endometriosis* by Susan M. Lark, M.D., *The Fibroid Book: A Guide to Treating the Most Common Cause of Hysterectomy* by Francis L. Hutchins, Jr., M.D., and *Healing Fibroids: A Doctor's Guide to a Natural Cure* by Allan Warshowsky, M.D. and Elena Oumano. However, I remained on the hunt for personal journeys written by women who actually struggled with symptomatic fibroids.

I needed points of reference from which to draw comparisons between my overwhelming symptoms and those of other women. I also needed confirmation that I wasn't the only woman stricken with what felt like the worst symptoms of this perplexing medical condition.

Pressed to write the kind of book I longed to read during my 15-year battle, five pounds of fibroids: a memoir is a candid account of what it's like living with symptomatic, uterine fibroid tumors. Explicitly unleashing my journey, this book reveals how fibroids affected my quality of life, sex life, relationships, career, and so much more.

Five pounds of fibroids: a memoir was also written to strike a chord within the medical community in hopes of advocating patient-centered, best practices in diagnosing, treating, and managing each woman's unique case of symptomatic fibroids; and prompt Congress in establishing an annual budget higher than the National Institutes of Health's current allotment for fibroid research.

Unearthing a range of emotions as I looked back on years of incomprehensible hell, I walked away from the manuscript several times. The eight-year writing process was so devastatingly difficult, I thought I would never finish it. However, a *force* kept pushing me to complete this book, so my story may shed some light on a disorder which causes some women's lives to turn upside down.

While living with symptomatic, uterine fibroid tumors was like not living at all, I am grateful to be alive. By sharing my plight, it is with hopes five pounds of fibroids: a memoir encourages women to speak openly about the subject; deters them from evading diagnosis and treatment out of shame, fear, or ignorance; educates women on the importance of personal research; empowers them to take aggressive action in partnering with health care providers concerning fibroid treatment options and management; and gives women peace of mind in knowing they are *not alone* in their battle against symptomatic, uterine fibroid tumors.

If you or someone you know suffers with debilitating symptoms of fibroids and are asking...

- How many more mattresses, chairs, couches, car and airplane seats am I going to destroy?
- Should I continue "*watching and waiting*" as my doctor recommends?
- Are large and multiple fibroids preventing me from

conceiving?

- Why are alternative and non-surgical treatments ineffective in treating my fibroids?
- Is hysterectomy my only option now that some of my fibroids are the size of grapefruit?
- Will my life be void of intimacy and sex considering fibroids have wreaked havoc in my past relationships?
- And, how much longer am I going to sit on the sidelines watching my life fall apart physically, psychologically, socially, and economically because of symptomatic, uterine fibroid tumors? Another year? Five years? Ten years? Fifteen years?

...read five pounds of fibroids: a memoir!

Rose Marie Johnson
Author, Sufferer, Survivor and Research Advocate

CHAPTER 1
Cataclysmic Crippling Cramps

Sharp Staggering Stabbings

Other than observing some sixth graders rubbing their stomachs during assembly; witnessing crying outbursts in the lunchroom; and seeing specks of blood on their shorts while playing in the schoolyard, I knew little about menstruation until it happened to me, at age 12.

Dressed in a pink and white short set with matching sneakers, I darted outside to play double-dutch with my friends. Although sweltering that early August afternoon in Brooklyn, New York, triple digit temperature didn't stop me from showing off my fancy foot moves and turning rope as fast as an eggbeater while chanting, *"Ten, twenty, thirty, forty, fifty, sixty, seventy, eighty, ninety, one-up. Two, three, four, five, six, seven, eight, nine, two-up…"*, at the top of my lungs.

Jumping in for what felt like the hundredth time and lifting my left knee to spin backwards, I looked downward and saw red spots in the center of my shorts. Believing I had torn something *down there* from jumping rope over an hour, double-dutch came to a screeching halt as I performed a *jump out* maneuver and hauled tail into the house.

In the bathroom, I pulled my shorts and multicolored *Monday* panties down to my ankles and stood gazing at the stains. Sitting on the toilet, stupefied, I yanked toilet paper from its roll. With my eyes closed, I began wiping my *private area* until brave enough to open them. And, after several minutes of nearly rubbing myself raw, I hopped off the toilet.

Covering the lower half of my body with my stained shorts, I opened the bathroom door and yelled, *"Is anyone there?"* Without any response, I ran a marathon's race up the flight of stairs and into my room. Grabbing a *dark* denim short set and panties from my dresser drawer, I headed toward the upstairs bathroom.

Afraid bathing would cause more blood to flow, I used a washcloth, soap, and water to clean myself instead. Snatching a hand mirror off the sink, I sat on the toilet to see if the bleeding had stopped. Nearly falling off the toilet seat as I looked at my private area for the first time in my life, I grabbed a fistful of toilet paper and placed it in the center of my panties. Pulling them over my hips, I stood glancing in the mirror to see if I were dead.

Although consumed with bleeding to death and terrified my friends may have also seen the bloodstains, I convinced myself that it was all a fleeting nightmare and went back to my room. After changing clothes, I headed down the stairs to resume jumping rope.

As I approached the landing, I looked between my legs to see if the bulk of toilet paper lodged in my panties was noticeable. In viewing what looked like a pair of balled-up socks protruding from my shorts, I ran upstairs and into my room once again. Overwhelmed by what was happening to me and out of sorts about wearing *Tuesday* panties considering it was still Monday, I sat on my bed and began crying.

In hearing my mother's angelic voice as she spoke with my grandmother on the phone, I contemplated whether I should barge into her room to announce my imminent death or wait for her to finish her conversation. But, as soon as I heard the handset hit the base, I inched toward her bedroom hoping she could help me with my *problem* and prevent me from dying.

When I reached her bedroom door, I tearfully blurted, *"Mommy, I saw blood in my shorts."* Taking me by the hand, she escorted me inside her room and closed the door. As I sat on her arm chair, she explained what menstruation was all about and what can happen if I had *hanky-panky* with boys now that I had become *'a beautiful young lady.'* And, in less than ten minutes, her warm, yet, direct birds and the bee's speech was over.

Reaching into her closet, she gave me a handful of sanitary pads and explained how to use them. She, then, demonstrated how to dispose of them by placing them inside plastic bags and shoving them to the bottom of the wastebasket or garbage can. After providing instructions on cleanliness; bathing more often than usual during *that time of the month*; and checking my pads every hour to avoid seepage, designating a *hiding place* to store them was the last order of business.

As we, mutually, decided to place them in the back of the built-in cabinet above the closet, I couldn't help from thinking why they needed to be hidden since I shared the bedroom with my two younger sisters. I could only assume menstruation was secretive and no one was to know I had begun my period. Not even my sisters.

Once our conversation about menstruation and boys was over, I resumed playing double-dutch padded to the hilt. Apparently, my friends hadn't a clue about my bloody ordeal and surely, I wasn't going to volunteer any information. However, overwhelmed with paranoia, I kept glancing between my legs to see if blood had escaped and darting to the bathroom every fifteen minutes or so to change pads. By evening, I had used all those my mother had given me and asked for another stash.

Feeling as if a volcano were erupting inside me, I struggled to fall asleep that night. The next morning, I awoke with a stomach ache and rubbery red balls resembling dried prunes sprawled on my pad. While seeing chunks of blood the width of dimes and nickels scared me to death, I was much too embarrassed to tell my mother, sisters or anyone. Thankfully, they disappeared after a few cycles.

Vaguely excited about puberty at age 12, I handled onset of menstruation and changing sanitary pads more often than I cared to fairly well. However, I was dealt an unfair hand when menstrual cramps appeared on the scene two years later.

Throbbing abdominal and pelvic pain usually began one or two days prior to my periods and ended on the fourth or fifth day of my cycles. In categorizing them based on level of intensity, *phase one crampisodes* were gut-churning and often felt like linebackers, donned in helmets, were ramming into my abdomen, pelvis and lower back.

If at school during this phase, I would take aspirin I customarily carried in my backpack. Waiting roughly an hour for pain to ease which always felt like an eternity, I would sit cradling my stomach and whimpering in silence.

When at home, I would take aspirin, lay in bed in the fetal position, and wait for pain which also felt like a swarm of killer bees inside me to subside. During this stage, I would try my best to grin and bear it knowing pain was bound to worsen shortly after onset of menstruation.

On the first day of my periods, I usually experienced intermittent twinges which was tolerable. However, on the second, third and fourth days which I referred as *phase two crampisodes*, pain felt like knives poking every organ in my pelvic, abdominal and lower back regions. Consuming aspirin and curling into the fetal position made little difference as insufferable spasms would subside whenever they felt like subsiding.

While menstrual cramps were, customarily, less painful during the last three days of my seven-day cycles, I often endured sour stomach and nausea which I attributed to the exorbitant amount of medication taken. Although I would coat my stomach with milk, crackers or a slice of bread prior, I still experienced sporadic throbbing which I called *phase three crampisodes.*

In junior high school, participating in sports and other activities when cramps were on a rampage was impossible. Often sitting on the bench squirming in pain and wondering why I seemed to be the only one plagued with bad cramps, I would watch as my classmates played net and field games. Gratefully, I had female physical education instructors who were aware of my battle and sympathetic. Had they been male, perhaps I would have failed PE classes considering the number of times I sat out.

While thrilled to perform in shows like *Pippin, Showboat, A Chorus Line*, and other productions during my junior high school years, all excitement vanished when cramps surfaced. In fact, I remember performing in a production of *The Wiz* with cramps so excruciating, I wanted to rip my stomach out. Had I known pain actually stemmed from my uterus, at the time, I would have wanted to yank that out also. However, I just dealt with it, as I was too embarrassed to ask the female music director or girls in the cast for pain relievers.

Throughout adolescence, menstrual cramps were so incapacitating, bedtime prayers consisted of the Lord's Prayer and begging God to change the timing of my periods so they'd always start on Fridays. Any time after school. This way, pain would be less piercing when I returned to school on Mondays. But, unable to defy the natural order of things, I would miss two or three days of school some months because of cramps.

With menstrual cramps progressively worsening throughout high school years, I often wished I had chosen a school closer to home. Living in Brooklyn and attending a performing arts high school in New York City, I spent an upward of three hours each day traveling back and forth. Rarely securing a seat on overcrowded buses and trains, I would stand clutching onto the iron handrails while writhing in stabbing pain, whenever cramps were on board.

Being late was out of the question as theatre students depended on each other for scene study and rehearsals. Therefore, on *I-wish-I-could-murder-my-cramps* mornings, I would arrive a half hour early. Heading straight to the restroom, I would sit on the toilet hoping pain medication would kick in before the bell rang.

Even while classes were in session, I would often dart out and seek refuge in the restroom when cramps felt like head-banging monsters inside my uterus. After taking more pain relievers, I would sit on the toilet with my arms wrapped around my stomach as I waited for the slightest break in pain. I'd, then, stumble back into class.

I remember the 50-something year old security guard who would check the girl's restroom every fifteen minutes or so to make sure we were all in class. Although stern with most students, she was warm and mother-like towards me. Oftentimes, she would knock on the bathroom door and ask, *"Are you okay, Rose?"* While I never figured out how she knew it was me, I could only assume she innately sensed I had *female problems*—considering how often she found me in the restroom while classes were in session.

Shortly after graduating from high school, I received a scholarship to study acting at a classical theatre conservatory in upstate New York. Elated to spend the summer sharpening my skills prior to attending university, I accepted. Upon arrival, however, I wanted to head back home with my parents.

Hidden in the boondocks, the compound-like environment with makeshift living quarters looked like prime location for a horror flick. Since I didn't grow up cohabiting with physically advantageous animals, I cowered every time I stepped out of my shack-like dorm room. Surely, rolling into the fetal position, playing dead, or running downhill to avert being attacked by grizzlies wasn't part of my modus operandi.

Living in the *wilderness* while on my period was also distressing. Although I packed a plethora of period paraphernalia including pain relievers, when stabbing cramps attacked, I felt like I was in purgatory. Forced to walk to and from outhouses that stood several yards away from my *shack*, especially at night, was equally anguishing and made cramps even worse.

Being in a strange environment with a hectic daily schedule and horrible cramps was so unnerving, I called my parents days later begging them to pick me up. As clueless as the instructors and students, they inquired as to why I wanted off the compound. And, I disguised the truth by stating I was bored—that I had already learned about Shakespeare, speech, diction, and dialects in high school. Although insufferable cramps were the main reason why I couldn't stay a day longer, I was too ashamed to talk to anyone about *my problem*. Not even my mother.

Venturing away from home again, at age 18, I attended a university in Purchase, New York to further my studies in acting. However, it seemed as if I were training for the Olympics. Since the theatre program required gymnastics several hours a week, performing cartwheels, somersaults and vaults especially while enduring atrocious cramps, would send my lower abdomen and pelvic area into shock. Therefore, fear of flunking gymnastics and other physically demanding classes led to withdrawal from the university within a year.

With dreadful cramps negatively affecting every aspect of my life, I was leery in accepting a scholarship at the prestigious theatre school in Valencia, California, at age 19. *"How, on earth, am I going to handle the heavy course load and physical requirements, for four years, with horrendous cramps."*, I thought.

Practically every day, I was required to take Tai Chi, a mind-body practice involving *"…certain postures and gentle movements with mental focus, breathing, and relaxation.'*[4] The slightest movement would exacerbate pain, tenfold, when stricken with cramps. And, regardless of consuming pain pills prior, sharp, organ-twisting cramps often caused me to dash out of class and into the restroom. Rocking back and forth with my face contorted, I'd sit on the toilet and pray that pain medication would quickly kick in so I could return to class.

To lessen the intensity of cramps during *shark week*, I began wearing corsets underneath my clothing. Familiar with being bound to the point of numbness when either rehearsing or performing in classical plays, I assumed regular wear would likely calm my wretched cramps. Unfortunately, it was either hit or miss, as strapping myself in like a tight seat belt sometimes helped. But, other times, it caused cramping pain to worsen.

Plagued with a uterus that went into charley horse mode a few days each month made college so challenging, I'm surprised I didn't drop out, entirely. I remember sitting in the middle of study

---

[4] "Tai Chi and Qi Gong: In Depth." *National Center for Complementary and Integrative Health*, www.nccih.nih.gov/health/taichi/introduction.htm#hed1.

hall, one morning, when teeth-clenching, scream-inducing cramps caused me to shoot out of my seat. Seeing the stunned look on my professor's face after uttering a few words during his opening lecture, he must've thought I was about to incite a protest.

As students seated in rows in front of me began turning around to see what all the commotion was about, I froze like a deer caught in headlights. Using my textbook and handbag as shields, I grasped my lower abdomen and limped out of study hall. Seeking refuge in the restroom, as was customary, I ransacked my handbag like a madwoman searching for pain medication.

Had I not been stigmatized with menstruation being a hush-hush, perhaps I would have felt comfortable pulling my professor aside and explaining, *"I'm really sorry I've disrupted your class, but I struggle with painful menstrual cramps. I'm in excruciating pain, at the moment, and can't seem to focus on anything except finding a way to make this pain go away."* However, I was much too ashamed to say anything and too embarrassed to return to class that morning.

Assuming menstruation was *secretive* since I neither heard any of my older sisters talk about their periods nor any discomfort they may have experienced, I didn't discuss my struggles with cyclical cramping pain with anyone either. I suppose growing up in a devout Christian household may have also played a role in why I suffered in silence from onset of my first period and throughout most of my adulthood. Knowing Leviticus 15:19-33, in the Bible, teaches a woman is considered *"unclean"*[5] when menstruating, I interpreted the passages to mean menstruation is on par with having a seven-day, infectious disease.

Perhaps, an addendum to the birds and bees' speech such, *'If at any time you experience cramps which causes you to ball over, cry, or vomit, let me know immediately. By doing so, pain can be temporarily treated with medication or medical advice sought to determine if there's some underlying disorder that's causing you discomfort.'*, may have encouraged me to speak openly about my struggle with cramps.

Throughout college, they were so debilitating, I regularly appeared in the nurse's office begging for medication to put me out

---

[5] *The Bible*. Authorized King James Version, Oxford University Press, 1998.

of misery. Often asked to describe my pain, I once told her, *"Cramps felt like weighted hooks being pierced through the innards of my vagina."*

Staring at me perplexed, she then asked something similar to, *"How can cramps be that painful?"* Considering how often I visited her office with complaints of horrible cramps, I was taken aback by her question. Apparently, she neither believed me nor followed basic principles of diagnosis as she'd handed me a three-month supply of birth control pills and sent me on my way.

Taking "the pill" for menstrual cramps, although formulated to prevent unwanted pregnancy always boggled my mind. Each time I'd push an *active* pill out of its socket, I couldn't help but think how ludicrous it was taking them while sexually inactive, at the time. However, noticing a decrease in pain by the third cycle, I was convinced birth control pills combined with over-the counter pain medication was the perfect cocktail in relieving cramps.

With pain less intense, I became more socially active and could tackle many of my normal daily routines like attending college classes. In fact, excessive absences dwindled as did the cycle of skipping out of classes and returning to my dorm room to curl into the fetal position until cramps subsided.

However, after a year or so of pain-free periods, seemingly, my body became resistant to birth control pills and low-dose pain medication. Landing back in the nurse's office with complaints of unbearable abdominal and pelvic pain, she swapped oral contraceptive brands and gave me prescription pain medication.

Not only were they both as ineffective as birth control pills and over-the-counter medication I had previously taken, my cramps became maddeningly worse and periods unpredictable. Never knowing when my cycles were going to start and stop, surely, I felt like a human feminine protection dispenser—as I was forced to carry a stockpile of tampons and sanitary pads at all times.

During another visit in which I was given gaggle of birth control pills and ibuprofen for cramps, surprisingly, the nurse offered me a work-study job overseeing the front office a few days a week. Being a golden opportunity for her to witness my physical response to brutal cramps and for me to receive proper treatment, I accepted and started several days later. Regrettably, an upgrade from ibuprofen to ineffective naproxen was all she'd give me for cramps.

After graduate school, cramps accompanied me into the workplace. When at work with a furious uterus, the thought of free falling off the top of office buildings I worked in seemed like the best *prescription* to end cramping misery. Instead, I would either remain in the restroom for long periods, request to leave early, or call out sick, especially when pain was equivalent to being a target at an archery range.

Inevitably raising red flags while working at a company for several years, I was often asked to explain my trend of lengthy restroom visits and absences which averaged two days per month. Accustomed to mentioning no more than *"I'm just having a terrible stomach ache"* or *"I'm a little under the weather"*, I finally divulged my history of debilitating cramps to my manager. In the same breath, I asked if I could go home an hour after clocking in because my uterus was throwing a temper tantrum.

Told I had to remain at work until the end of my shift made clear how some view menstrual cramps as a minor, fleeting issue easily overcome with pain medication. Choosing my well-being over her insensitivity towards my hard-to-treat cramps, I headed back to my desk to collect my belongings. And, as I left the office, the thought of giving two-week's notice never crossed my mind.

Since health care providers could neither adequately treat nor find the culprit of my problematic menstrual cramps, I engrossed myself in medical books, journals, and other types of literature. I was both desperate and determined to find answers as to what was causing agonizing cramps and how to best treat them since pain medication and birth control pills couldn't cut the mustard.

Bombarded with convoluted medical jargon that only those with Doctor of Medicine degrees could comprehend, I had to attach a dictionary and thesaurus to my hip. After learning intermittent piercing pain experienced in the abdomen, pelvic region and lower back just before and/or during menstruation were common symptoms of *dysmenorrhea,* meaning *"pain associated with menstruation"* [6], my next step entailed figuring out which of the three types of dysmenorrhea I likely had.

---

[6] "Dysmenorrhea: Painful Periods." FAQ 046. *ACOG*, 2015, www.acog.org/Patients/FAQs/Dysmenorrhea-Painful-Periods.

According to the American College of Obstetricians and Gynecologists, *"Primary dysmenorrhea is pain that comes from having a menstrual period, or 'menstrual cramps'."*[7] It's usually *"…caused by natural chemicals called prostaglandins…made in the lining of the uterus."*[8] And, when levels of these chemicals are in excess, they are known to cause "frequent and dysrhythmic" [9] contractions or cramps during menstruation.

Secondary dysmenorrhea is painful menstruation *"…caused by a disorder in the reproductive system"*[10] such as endometriosis and uterine fibroid tumors. And, *membranous dysmenorrhea*, is a severe form of secondary dysmenorrhea which *"involves the spontaneous slough of the endometrium in one cylindrical or membranous piece that retains the shape of the*

---

[7] "Dysmenorrhea: Painful Periods." FAQ 046. *ACOG*, 2015, www.acog.org/Patients/FAQs/Dysmenorrhea-Painful-Periods.

[8] "Dysmenorrhea: Painful Periods." FAQ 046. *ACOG*, 2015, www.acog.org/Patients/FAQs/Dysmenorrhea-Painful-Periods.

[9] Dawood, MY. "Primary Dysmenorrhea: Advances in Pathogenesis and Management." *Obstet Gynecol*, Aug. 2006, Vol.108, no. 2, pp. 428-441, *National Center for Biotechnology Information*, www.ncbi.nlm.nih.gov/pubmed/16880317, Abstract.

[10] "Dysmenorrhea: Painful Periods." FAQ 046. *ACOG*, 2015, www.acog.org/Patients/FAQs/Dysmenorrhea-Painful-Periods.

uterine cavity."[11] When the membranous piece or *decidual*, *endometrial* or *uterine cast* passes through the cervix, intense cramping pain can occur.[12]

Clearly a member of the *Dysmenorrhea Club*, I shared my research efforts with health care providers who would espouse over and over, *"menstrual cramps are normal."* Instead of ordering standard tests such as ultrasound (scanning of the womb and pelvis) or laparoscopy (examination of internal organs of the pelvis using a telescope)[13] to identify any underlying uterine abnormalities that could be responsible for unbearable cramping pain, school nurses, family physicians and gynecologists would continually prescribe what seemed like a lifetime supply of pain medication and birth control pills as treatment for my harrowing cramps.

---

[11] Rabinerson, D., Kaplan B., et al. "Membranous Dysmenorrhea: The Forgotten Entity." *Obstet Gynecol*, May 1995, Vol. 85, no. 5 Pt 2, pp. 891-892, www.doi.org/10.1016/0029-7844(94)00302-T, Abstract.
[12] Pingili, R. and Jackson, W. "Decidual Cast." *The Internet Journal of Gynecology and Obstetrics*, 2007, Vol. 9, no.1, www.ispub.com/IJGO/9/1/11420, Abstract.
[13] "Dysmenorrhea: Painful Periods." FAQ 046. *ACOG*, 2015, www.acog.org/Patients/FAQs/Dysmenorrhea-Painful-Periods.

Heat as Hot as Hades

Since birth control pills and prescription medication couldn't restrain pain that was equivalent to a throng of racehorses stampeding on my abdomen, pelvis, and lower back, I used a variety of heat-based products in attempt to zap cramps into oblivion. In fact, I should've been a spokeswoman for leading manufacturers of menstrual heating pads, bags and wraps, considering how frequently I used them when in the throes of sharp, shooting pain.

Throughout university years, writhing and moaning on dormitory floors with hot contraptions stuck to my gut and back was the norm. Lying on industrial carpet, prior to and during menstruation, was far more comfortable than the ultra-thin, coil-protruding dorm mattresses. However, during my first semester of college, my ritual in coping with cramps met resistance by two of my dorm mates who, luckily, had *normal periods*.

I suppose seeing me either thrashing about the floor or passed out looking like a giant burrito with heating gadgets wrapped around me, was likely the reason why one of them moved out. The last to depart filed a complaint with the residence director.

Fed up with finding me cowered on the floor whimpering in pain, especially at night, she claimed I prevented her from sleeping which caused her to be late to her morning classes. She also alleged I was using drugs.

Floored when informed of the grievance and asked if I needed drug intervention by the director, I revealed my ongoing struggles with painful menstruation. I also informed her about my *drug use* which consisted of ibuprofen and naproxen, both of which did little for my torturous cramps. Though appearing concerned, she had the audacity to tell me I needed to be considerate of my dorm mate by lying in my bed instead of on the floor when ill. Utterly baffled, I requested a transfer to another dorm room. However, my dorm mate had beaten me to the punch and moved out the next day.

Before my new dorm mate could unpack, I straightforwardly enlightened her about my cramping horrors and various ways in which I coped. Sharing her plight with painful menstruation not only caused a sigh of relief, I was confident she wouldn't file a complaint against me as my previous dorm mate had.

During the first few months as dorm mates, our cycles were

approximately two weeks apart until *menstrual synchrony* gradually sat in. A phenomenon first researched by Martha McClintock in 1971, menstrual synchrony suggests some women who cohabitate over a period of time, without male presence, give off scents called *pheromones* that can trigger onset of menstruation within days apart.[14] Although the theory has met criticism in medical reviews and subsequent studies, my dorm mate and I, undoubtedly, experienced what's coined the *McClintock Effect*.

As we began menstruating a day or two apart, it seemed like our cramping pain attacks were also synchronized. Spending several hours a month cooped up in our dorm room; wallowing in pain with heating gadgets strapped to our bellies and backs; and swallowing pain pills like miniature mints, was as pitiful as it gets. Inevitably, menstrual synchrony transformed us into *witch mates*. Unable to tolerate each other's hormonal fluctuations, gripes and groans, we both requested dorm mate changes at the end of the second semester.

---

[14] McClintock, MK. "Menstrual Synchrony and Suppression." *Nature*, 22 Jan. 1971, Vol. 229, no 5282, pp. 244-245, www.dx.doi.org/10.1038/229244a0.

After graduate school, I continued strapping hot contraptions onto my abdomen and back as painful menstruation worsened. Enduring cramps which felt like my uterus was being flung into a paper shredder several days a month, it's surprising I lasted as long as I did while working as a computer instructor. Experiencing relentless cramps while teaching was so grueling, I often wished I had the gift of Jeannie so I could disappear behind the movable whiteboard; pop a pain pill or two; affix a heating contraption, and resume teaching within a blink of an eye.[15]

I remember teaching an eight-hour advanced spreadsheets class at a company, in pain so intense, I wanted to rip my uterus out with my bare hands. Although I consumed two prescription pain relievers prior to leaving home, upon arrival my womb still felt like it was rubbing against a metal washboard. Afraid of overdosing by taking more medication minutes before the start of class, I taught the first four hours silently bawling in front of approximately fifteen employees.

---

[15] *I Dream of Jeannie*, written by Sidney Sheldon, directed by Gene Nelson, Hal Cooper, and Claudio Guzman, performances by Barbara Eden, Larry Hagman, Bill Daily, and Hayden Rorke, Sony Pictures Television, 1965.

Staggering out of the building and into the back seat of my car, during my one-hour lunch break, I ripped open a box of an air-activated, heat wrap patches that I usually carried in my handbag. As I waited roughly twenty minutes for it to warm up, I swallowed two more pain relievers hoping medication and heat would make cramps quickly subside, so I could teach the second half of the class. Once attached to my lower abdomen, I curled into the fetal position and dozed off for forty-five minutes.

Struck by sharp, grinding cramps which felt like my vaginal innards were entangled in a thorn bush, a few hours after class resumed, I felt like launching into a cramps-cursing tirade. Considering the inappropriateness in doing so, I sped through the remaining topics and ended class thirty minutes earlier than scheduled.

Hastily turning off the computers and tidying up the classroom, I rushed to my car, plopped on the back seat, assumed the fetal position, and slept over two hours. Miraculously, my long cramp-filled day resulted in glowing class evaluations. And, I avoided rush hour traffic too.

While disposable heating pads and wraps afforded

temporary peace from pain, they often caused allergic reactions. Seemingly containing bomb-making ingredients, I would end up with burns which felt like ghost peppers had been smeared onto them. Therefore, I stopped using store-bought heating pads and wraps and made my own natural-based, heating paraphernalia, instead.

In preparing homemade heating pads, I would fill a pair of tube socks with uncooked rice, Garbanzo or Kidney beans and flaxseeds. After adding a dash of either peppermint or lavender oil for fragrance and spritzing the concoction with water for moisture, I would tie the open ends into knots. Then, in the microwave they'd go for two minutes, with a cup of water to prevent fires.

As hot as coals and heavy as barbells, I would protect my skin with hand towels. Lying in bed or on the floor, I'd place one on my abdomen and the other underneath my lower back. While the heat and weight of my *hot socks* helped soothe cramps and prevented skin irritation, they cooled quicker than manufactured heating products. Making frequent trips to the kitchen to re-heat them, especially when savage cramps struck in the middle of the night, became much too labor-intensive. Therefore, I'd use other methods to calm cramps.

Old-fashioned, hot water bottles were often used in my ongoing battle against cramps. I would fill two red rubbery jugs with near-boiling water, place them inside pillowcases, and lay them on my abdomen and lower back. Although intense heat felt soothing, initially, it would dissipate after a few minutes. Therefore, I had to constantly boil water and refill the bottles which was as high maintenance as nuking socks.

Discovering electric heating pads were more effective than water bottles and tube socks filled with rice, beans and grains, I armed myself with two extra-large pads. In fact, I kept one on my nightstand and the other on the armchair in my living room for quick access when in cramping turmoil. As soon as belligerent cramps surfaced, I'd wrap a pad around my abdomen and back and plug it into the nearest socket.

Though I felt like a mummy, deep penetrating heat would suppress violent cramps quicker than other heat-based products. The only drawback was the toxic-smelling stench that would emit shortly after plugging it in. Reeking of fumes from either plastic or gel fillers embedded inside the pad, the smell of burnt shower curtains would linger in the air for hours. Unable to quash the foul odor with aerosol spray or scented candles, I would set it near an open window to air out for several hours.

Unlike disposable pads, I could manually control the temperature of electric heating pads. However, when set on high, I feared dozing off and waking up charred or not at all. As a matter of fact, I once fell asleep wrapped in an electric heating pad and awoke the next morning to a mid-section hotter than miso soup. Shooting out of bed and seeing a singed area on my bedsheet, I immediately unstrapped the electric pad. Luckily, I only sustained a blister on my belly and smelled of burnt chemicals.

Instead of exchanging it for another, I stopped using electric heating pads to treat cramps altogether. While I could've tolerated the repulsive smell, chancing a mattress meltdown, second degree burns, or death would have been asinine. Therefore, I used less hazardous forms of heat therapy although they weren't as effective.

Plain hot water bottles would sometimes take the edge off, especially when experiencing harrowing cramps at work. I remember sitting at my desk, one morning, in pain so paralyzing I was tempted to crawl into the fetal position under it. Forgetting the liter of bottled water at home, I drove to the nearest convenience store during my lunch break to buy one. Upon returning, I tossed it into the microwave for approximately five minutes. Racing to the restroom, I sat on the toilet and held it against my pelvis for relief.

Considering I had a few minutes left of my lunch break, I went back to my desk and popped two more pain pills, hoping to get through the rest of day agony-free. However, within an hour of resuming work, throbbing pain returned with such vengeance, I microwaved the water bottle a second time and off to the restroom I went to doctor my cramps.

When struck with cruel cramps, the sauna became my sanctuary. I frequented it, while living on campus at a college I attended, hoping to steam my cramps away. Continuously pouring water on the volcanic-like stones to draw as much heat as possible, I would sit on the top wooden row of the small, co-ed sauna in my bathing suit, with a towel draped around my lower half.

Whenever alone in the sauna, I could moan aloud until steam penetrated the cramping areas of my body. However, my ritual usually turned vexatious when other students were present. As a case in point, I remember impatiently waiting for my last class to end so I could slay my spine-bending cramps with steam. In opening the door and seeing two students whom I knew, I was tempted to yell fire. Perhaps, I should have after listening to their conversation as agonizing as the pain I was in. Instead, I exited and waited over thirty minutes for them to vacate.

Surprisingly, I never ended up with heat stroke considering how often I took saunas to ease cramping pain. Spending fifteen to twenty-minutes, once or twice a day, did cause heavier blood flow, however. To avoid raging periods, I limited sauna use and began wearing sauna suits.

Although designed to burn calories, melt pounds, and remove toxins, I would hop into my silver or cobalt sauna suit in attempts to thwart cramping pain. But, unfortunately, wearing them for hours at a time did nothing more than cause light-headedness and dehydration. Knowing I'd be at a loss for words explaining to emergency room personnel why I habitually wore sauna suits, I thought it best to steer clear of them.

In sharing the many ways I coped with horrendous cramps with a friend who also suffered with them, she recommended sitz baths. Although I had never heard of the hydrotherapy treatment claiming to relieve pain associated with painful menstruation, uterine fibroids and other medical conditions[16], I was willing to try anything.

Therefore, over the next two or three cycles, I would fill the bathtub with three to four inches of warm water. After adding Epsom salt, I'd sit in the tub with my knees bent upward so that cramping areas were immersed in water for roughly fifteen minutes.

Sometimes, I would alternate between taking traditional sitz baths and using a sitz bath bowl. While I found the latter process awkward because it entailed placing the plastic bowl on the rim of toilet; filling it with warm water; and dunking my derrière and vagina, or *perineum* in it for fifteen minutes or so, I did it as recommended and out of desperation.

I supposed the only upside to *sitzing* on the bowl was squeezing warm water on my pelvis using the plastic bag and tubing that came with the kit. Surely, it helped substantially in taking the edge off deep crushing cramps. However, the bowl didn't have

---

[16] Conner K. "The Sitz Bath in Gynecology." *Naturopathic Doctor News & Review*, 1 Feb. 2009, www.ndnr.com/womens-health/the-sitz-bath-in-gynecology.

a hole so that excess water could flow into the toilet, like other brands. Therefore, I'd end up with a puddle of water on the floor—not to mention loosened grout around the base.

I also explored vaginal steam baths. Known as *yonis*, vaginal steaming is an ancient healing practice that's used in many cultures and purports to ease menstrual cramps, cleanse the vagina of impurities, and increase blood circulation.[17]

To avoid the expense of hiring a yoni steam practitioner to humidify my womb, I would bring about a half-gallon of water combined with either basil, oregano leaves, calendula, chamomile or other dried herbs to a boil. After pouring contents into a metal basin with handles and placing it inside the toilet, I would drape myself in a blanket from the waist down, lower myself onto the *hot seat*, and pray an earthquake wouldn't erupt during the process.

With a pot of herbs stewing in close proximity to my lady parts for twenty to forty minutes, made my vagina feel as if it were on fire. Forced to either sway from side to side to let some steam

---

[17] Nall, R. "What to Know About Vaginal Steaming." Reviewed by Ernst, H., 1 Aug. 2018, *MedicalNewsToday*, www.medicalnewstoday.com/articles/322657.php.

out or hop off the toilet to fasten a cold compress to it, vaginal steaming was the most unnerving remedy I experimented with. Perhaps, yonis may have worked wonders in taming my cramps had I been able to tolerate steam as hot as a furnace.

Whenever my usual heating remedies and therapies failed to put me out of misery, I would resort boiling or microwaving washcloths. Using tongs to remove them from the pot or plastic bag, I would put them on a plate to cool. Once the temperature was bearable, I'd place them on my abdomen, pelvis and back for relief. But, much like hot socks and water bottles, washcloths would cool within minutes causing me to repeat the process a number of times to gain some relief.

Short of stacking hot tortillas on my pain-riddled belly and pelvis, I would sometimes attempt ironing my vicious cramps away. After layering the areas with a bath towel; pouring water into the compartment; and setting the temperature on high, I would press the steam button. Upon seeing miniature bubbles percolate through the holes, I'd iron away as if ironing a pair of jeans.

While the intensity of heat and pressure often helped in diminishing pain, I wouldn't recommend using an iron for purposes other than its intended use. In retrospect, had I shared such drastic measure with health care providers, surely, they would have ordered a straitjacket and extended stay at an insane asylum.

Using an overheating laptop was another desperate means of coping with painful menstruation. Resting it on my lower abdomen for an hour or so would sometimes minimize pain. Even though radiating heat caused relentless itching, the benefits seemed to outweigh the discomfort. However, later learning exposure to non-ionizing radiation in laptops can potentially cause infertility and cancer, I halted use immediately.[18]

I would also use my electric body massager hoping to massage cramps away, especially when they were exasperating and other remedies couldn't relieve them. Setting the temperature on high, I'd lie on my back gliding infrared light waves, heat, and vibration over my abdomen and pelvis. However, habitually falling asleep with the large wand on top of my pelvis and waking up hours later with it lodged elsewhere, hotter than a butane blow torch,

---

[18] Bellieni, CV., Pinto, I., et al. "Exposure to Electromagnetic Fields from Laptop Use of "Laptop" Computers." *Arch Environ Occup Health*, 2012, Vol. 67, no. 1, pp. 31-6, *PubMed*, www.ncbi.nlm.nih.gov/pubmed/22315933, Abstract.

proved more hazardous than beneficial. To prevent both injury and electrocution, I'd only use the body massager when sitting upright and awake.

In conjunction with most heat therapies and medications, I drank hot fluids to aid in obliterating my awful cramps. Bringing either ginger root, rosemary, chamomile, peppermint leaves, or even plain water to a boil, I'd drink approximately three to four cups days prior and during my periods. Although I'd grimace with each sip, drinking hot liquids was worth the tongue and throat torture—as cramps would eventually ease, temporarily.

From birth control pills to vaginal steaming, I experimented with a plethora of remedies to control my revolting cramps. With pain either dissipating for a short period or not at all, my uterus, lower abdomen and back usually felt like they were in the mouth of a crocodile.

Cramps were so relentless, I was literally scared of them. In fact, I compared my menstrual cramping mayhem to the title of the horror film *Invasion of the Body Snatchers*—as they *invaded* my body and *snatched* away my life.[19] It's no wonder I developed an affinity towards gory movies and books throughout years of suffering in menstrual hell. I not only became an avid enthusiast of writers of horror, I wrote several spine-tingling synopses and scripts as a cathartic way of dealing with my own *horrors*.

---

[19] *Invasion of the Body Snatchers*, based on novel written by Jack Finney, directed by Phillip Kaufman, performances by Donald Sutherland, Brooke Adams, Leonard Nimoy, Jeff Goldblum and Veronica Cartwright, United Artists, 1978.

Narcotics Needed, Now!

Menstrual cramps felt like a pair of pit bulls munching on my uterus as if a doggie treat. With complaints of ineffective prescription medication and birth control pills falling on deaf ears, I was willing to cavort with the devil in exchange for opioids. However, a college boyfriend and health fanatic suggested I shelve the narcotics idea and first explore a vegan diet.

Adamant in his belief that consumption of red meat and non-organic food increases the risk of gynecological disorders, heart disease and other conditions, I eventually embraced veganism. As I swapped processed food for organic and eliminated meat, poultry, fish, eggs and dairy, I made sure I consumed recommended dietary allowances of essential vitamins.

To maintain a healthy immune system, I ate romaine lettuce, kale, broccoli, arugula, spinach and other dark leafy vegetables that are loaded with beta-carotene, a natural antioxidant used by the body in producing vitamin A.[20] I also consumed orange and

---

[20] "Vitamin A." U.S. National Library of Medicine, 2 Apr. 2015. *MedlinePlus*, www.medlineplus.gov/vitamina.html.

yellow fruits and vegetables including cantaloupe, grapefruit, mangos, carrots, and sweet potatoes.

In meeting daily values of vitamin C, an antioxidant which assists in the growth and repair of all bodily parts, supports the body's absorption of iron, and promotes healthy skin, bones and teeth[21], I ate red and green peppers, tomatoes, broccoli, papaya, strawberries, and citrus fruits. I also drank organic citrus juices.

My intake of vitamin D which helps the body absorb calcium needed for development of healthy bones, regulates the immune system and cells, and maintains calcium and phosphorous blood levels[22], was acquired through daily exposure to sunlight. I also took 5000 IUs of cholecalciferol supplements as recommended by health care providers.

To satisfy recommended dietary allowances of vitamin E, *"an antioxidant that plays a role in your immune system and metabolic processes"*[23], I ate green vegetables, wheat germ,

---

[21] "Vitamin C." U.S. National Library of Medicine, 2 Apr. 2015. *MedlinePlus*, www.medlineplus.gov/vitaminc.html.
[22] "Vitamin D." U.S. National Library of Medicine, 26 Mar. 2015. *MedlinePlus*, www.medlineplus.gov/vitamind.html.
[23] "Vitamin E." U.S. National Library of Medicine, 2 Apr. 2015. *MedlinePlus*, www.medlineplus.gov/vitamine.html.

almonds, sunflower seeds, and olive, sunflower and safflower vegetable oils. And, vitamin K intake consisted of Brussels sprouts, cauliflower, cabbage and kale, all of which aids in the growth and development of the body *"by making proteins for healthy bones and tissues."*[24]

Eating foods within the vitamin B family was initially challenging since there are eight types. But, after understanding the purposes and benefits of each through research, my intake of vitamin B1 or *thiamin* which *"helps the body's cells change carbohydrates into energy"* and provides *"energy for the body, especially the brain and nervous system"*[25] included bananas, mushrooms, spinach, seaweed, green beans, peas, broccoli, avocado, yams, and nuts.

For vitamin B2 or *riboflavin* which is *"...important for body growth and red blood cell production"*, and *"...releasing of energy from proteins"*[26], I consumed soybeans, tempeh, spinach,

---

[24] "Vitamin K." U.S. National Library of Medicine, 2 Apr. 2015. *MedlinePlus*, www.medlineplus.gov/vitamink.html.
[25] "Thiamin." U.S. National Library of Medicine, 1 Oct. 2018. *MedlinePlus*, www.medlineplus.gov/ency/article/002401.htm.
[26] "Riboflavin." U.S. National Library of Medicine, 1 Oct. 2018. *MedlinePlus*, www.medlineplus.gov/ency/article/002411.htm.

mushrooms, cauliflower, Brussels sprouts, squash, asparagus, and almonds. Intake of vitamin B3 or *niacin* which is beneficial in *"...preventing premenstrual headache, improving digestion, protecting against toxins and pollutants..."*[27] included wheat, rice, celery leaves, mushrooms, cantaloupe, mangos, and peaches.

For B5 or *pantothenic acid* which allows the body *"...to properly use carbohydrates, proteins, and lipids and for healthy skin"*[28], I ate Shitake mushrooms, sweet potatoes, lentils, dried peas, and avocados. For vitamin B6 or *pyridoxine* which the body requires for *"...utilization of energy in the foods you eat, production of red blood cells, and proper functioning of nerves"*[29], I ate corn, wheat bran, potatoes, and spinach. For vitamin B7 or *biotin* which is *"...commonly used for hair loss, brittle nails, nerve damage, and many other conditions"*[30], I ate soybeans, nuts, and yeast.

Since daily allowances of vitamin B8 or *inositol* which is

---

[27] "Niacin." U.S. National Library of Medicine, 27 Jul. 2018. *MedlinePlus*, www.medlineplus.gov/druginfo/natural/924.html.
[28] "Pantothenic Acid." U.S. National Library of Medicine, 17 Sep. 2018. *MedlinePlus*, www.medlineplus.gov/druginfo/natural/853.html.
[29] "Pyridoxine." U.S. National Library of Medicine, 22 Oct. 2018. *MedlinePlus*, www.medlineplus.gov/druginfo/meds/a682587.html.
[30] "Biotin." U.S. National Library of Medicine, 17 Sep. 2018. *MedlinePlus*, www.medlineplus.gov/druginfo/natural/313.html.

used to *"balance certain chemicals in the body"*[31] has yet to be established, I was least concerned about this particular B vitamin. To ensure my body was getting adequate daily values of vitamin B9 or *folic acid* which *"...helps the body make healthy new cells"*[32], I ate collard and mustard greens, broccoli, tomatoes, spinach, lentils, Garbanzo and Pinto beans, and parsley. For vitamin B12 or *cyanocobalamin* which *"...is important for protein metabolism"* and *"helps in the formation of red blood cells and in the maintenance of the central nervous system"*[33], I consumed probiotic and enzyme salads, nutritional yeast, sea vegetables, and vitamin B12 supplements.

Getting enough protein, a nutrient that's necessary *"...to build and maintain bones, muscles and skin"*[34] was tough since I didn't eat meat, eggs, dairy and other non-vegan foods. However, consuming organic tofu and tempeh, both of which are good

---

[31] "Inositol." Natural Medicines Comprehensive Database Consumer Version. Therapeutic Research Faculty, 2018, *WebMD*, www.webmd.com/vitamins/ai/ingredientmono-299/inositol.

[32] "Folic Acid." U.S. National Library of Medicine, 23 Oct. 2018. *MedlinePlus*, www.medlineplus.gov/folicacid.html.

[33] "Vitamin B12." U.S. National Library of Medicine, 1 Oct. 2018. *MedlinePlus*, www.medlineplus.gov/ency/article/002403.htm.

[34] "Dietary Proteins." U.S. National Library of Medicine, 31 Jan. 2018. *MedlinePlus*, www.medlineplus.gov/dietaryproteins.html.

sources of protein, enabled me to meet daily recommended allowances.[35] I also ate oatmeal, quinoa, whole wheat bread, lentils, and brown rice; and regularly drank protein smoothies containing wheat grass, spinach, chia and hemp seeds.

While there were noticeable improvements in my overall health including heightened energy, increased metabolism, weight loss, and skin suppleness, my vegan lifestyle and consumption of supplements, for over three years, neither stopped nor reduced the intensity of maddening cramps.

Determined to find a cure, my boyfriend then suggested I take herbs and botanicals. With the input of herbalists, he worked alongside, he recommended Dong Quai, *"…an herb native to China, Japan, and Korea"* that is *"…useful for replenishing and invigorating blood, relieving pain, and moistening the intestines, resulting in its application for the treatment of menstrual disorders…"*[36]

---

[35] Wang, HL. "Tofu and Tempeh as Potential Protein Sources in the Western Diet." *JAOCS*, 1984, Vol. 61, pp. 528-534. *Wiley Online Library*, www.onlinelibrary.wiley.com/doi/abs/10.1007/BF02677023, Abstract.

[36] Fang, L., Xiao, X-F., et al. "Recent Advance in Studies on Angelica Sinensis." *Chin. Herb. Med*, 2012, Vol. 4, p. 12, doi:10.3969/j.issn.1674-6384.2012.01.004, Abstract.

Sold on the idea, I took one 550 milligram capsule of Dong Quai root daily. By the third cycle, cramps were markedly less agonizing. Instead of lying in the fetal position for hours on end during my cycles, I was able to move about the planet like women with *normal* periods. However, by the fourth or fifth cycle, the herbal supplement lost its effectiveness and full-blown cramps returned.

Although skeptical, I continued riding the herbal bandwagon experimenting with a variety of other supplements touting to relieve painful menstruation. In so doing, I explored blue cohosh, a supplement that claims to treat cramps and several other conditions.[37] Failing to lessen pain after consuming the herb for over three or four cycles, I then experimented with yarrow, an herb that's said to contain *"...chemicals that might help to stop stomach cramps and fight infections."*[38] However, it actually caused stomach upset which exacerbated menstrual cramps.

I, then, tried cramp bark, an herb purporting to relieve

---

[37] "Blue Cohosh." Natural Medicines Comprehensive Database Consumer Version. Therapeutic Research Faculty, 2018, *WebMD*, www.webmd.com/vitamins/ai/ingredientmono-987/blue-cohosh.
[38] "Yarrow." Natural Medicines Comprehensive Database Consumer Version. Therapeutic Research Faculty, 2018, *WebMD*, www.webmd.com/vitamins/ai/ingredientmono-151/yarrow.

cramps *"...including muscle spasms, menstrual cramps, and cramps during pregnancy."*[39] Without positive results after consuming the herb twice a day, for approximately two cycles, I explored false unicorn root, an herb used for *"...menstrual problems"*[40] among other symptoms and conditions. However, like most herbs, false unicorn root didn't reduce cramping pain after three or four months of use.

Jumping on the herbal tea bandwagon hoping herbs infused with flowers, leaves, seeds, and roots would decrease pain, I must have tried every type of tea on the market. Alleging to ease menstrual cramps, I went tea-crazy experimenting with birch, black haw, Echinacea, sassafras, and several others.

With raspberry leaf tea being the most effective in lessening painful menstruation, I drank it like water. In fact, three days prior to onset and throughout my length of my periods, I'd sip at least four cups a day. However, when what I deemed a miracle tea for

---

[39] "Cramp Bark." Natural Medicines Comprehensive Database Consumer Version. Therapeutic Research Faculty, 2018, *WebMD*, www.webmd.com/vitamins/ai/ingredientmono-746/cramp-bark.

[40] "False Unicorn." Natural Medicines Comprehensive Database Consumer Version. Therapeutic Research Faculty, 2018, *WebMD*, www.webmd.com/vitamins/ai/ingredientmono-193/false-unicorn.

cramps lost effectiveness after three months of use, I was devastated.

Seemingly immune to most herbs and herbal teas some women with problematic menstruation rave about, I became leery of herbal products. Later learning some products contain toxic metals that can cause lethal side effects after viewing websites such as consumerlab.com, an online database that rates herbs for quality; and fda.gov that reports safety information, adverse reaction warnings, and recalls of herbal remedies and vitamins under the Food and Drug Administration's MedWatch program, I stopped consuming herbal products entirely.

Venturing back into the self-help wilderness to find ways to control cramps, I turned to *complementary and alternative medicine (CAM)*, an assortment of medical and health care systems, practices, and products. Emphasizing *"a holistic, patient-focused approach to health care and wellness—often including mental, emotional, functional, spiritual, social, and community aspects—and treating the whole person rather than, for example, one organ system."*[41] gave me a glimmer of hope and I began reading books on CAM including *Treating Menstrual Cramps Naturally: Effective Natural Solutions for Discomforts Most Women Face* by Susan M. Lark, M.D., *The Complementary and Alternative Medicine Information Source Book* by Alan M. Rees, *The American Holistic Medical Association Guide to Holistic Health: Healing Therapies for Optimal Wellness* by Larry Trivieri, Jr., and *The Complete Book of Ayurvedic Home Remedies* by Vasant Lad, B.A.M.S, M.A.Sc.

In learning a great deal and viewing statistics which shows, *"Many Americans—more than 30 percent of adults and about 12 percent of children—use health care approaches that are not typically part of conventional medical care or that may have origins outside of usual Western practice."*[42], I was eager to explore acupressure, one of several bodywork therapies which uses *"fingers, palms, elbows or feet, or special devices to apply pressure*

---

[41] "Complementary, Alternative, or Integrative Health: What's in a Name?" National Center for Complimentary and Integrative Health, 8 Nov. 2018, www.nccih.nih.gov/health/integrative-health.

[42] "Complementary, Alternative, or Integrative Health: What's in a Name?" National Center for Complimentary and Integrative Health, 8 Nov. 2018, www./nccih.nih.gov/health/integrative-health.

to acupoints on the body's meridians."[43], for my painful periods and to possibly uncover any underlying culprit.

Prior to experimenting with acupressure, I asked my doctor if the complementary treatment combined with prescription medication would be an effective way to reduce the level of pain I usually experienced. Responding with something similar to, *"Acupressure may not be effective, long-term, and can possibly cause other medical issues"*, I was at my wits end.

Desperate and willing to give it a shot, I sought the aid of an acupressure practitioner experienced in Tui Na, a vigorous form of Chinese bodywork combining acupressure, massage and other types of bodily manipulation, anyway.[44] Lying face down on the massage table, the practitioner would perform the oscillating technique which entailed rapid rolling of thumbs and knuckles over my lower back and shoulders to improve circulation.

However, high-frequency kneading felt more like a spinal

---

[43] "Acupressure Points and Massage Treatment." WebMD Medical Reference, 21 Oct. 2017, Reviewed by Kiefer, D., *WebMD*, www.webmd.com/balance/guide/acupressure-points-and-massage-treatment#1.
[44] Yang, M., Feng, Y., et al. "Effectiveness of Chinese Massage Therapy (Tui Na) for Chronic Low Back Pain: Study Protocol for a Randomized Controlled Trial." *Trials*, 29 Oct. 2014, Vol. 15, no. 418, doi:10.1186/1745-6215-15-418, Abstract.

beatdown than therapeutic bodywork. In fact, I'd cringe each time I was instructed to flip over onto my back so pressure could be applied to *acupoints* around my stomach region. Although I'd try to inhale and exhale through the pressure, as suggested, my body never reacted positively. Therefore, the third Tui Na session was my last, as I sensed the practitioner was attempting beat the cramps out of me.

I, then, explored Shiatsu which *"...uses finger pressure, manipulations and stretches, along Traditional Chinese Medicine meridians."*[45] Wearing loose fitting clothing during each session, I'd lay on a futon as the practitioner gently massaged the web between my thumb and forefinger to trigger blood circulation. After applying pressure to points on my feet, using small circular movements, she'd place her palm and fingertips on my sacrum, the large bony area at the base of the spine, for several seconds.

Flipping over onto my back midway during the thirty-minute sessions, the practitioner would apply pressure to *meridians* or

---

[45] Robinson N., Lorenc, A., et al. "The Evidence for Shiatsu: A Systemic Review of Shiatsu and Acupressure." *BMC Complement Altern Med*, 7 Oct. 2011, Vol. 11, no. 88, doi:10.1186/1472-6882-11-88, Abstract.

channels below my naval. Holding the point for three to five seconds and instructing me to take deep breaths, muscle tension and pain would slowly yield to the pressure. And, cramps would temporarily subside shortly after each session.

I also experimented with Jin Shin Jyutsu, *"a gentle form of acupressure therapy that uses light finger pressure over specific points."*[46] During the hour-long sessions, I'd lay on a cushioned table as the facilitator first listened to energy pulses in my wrists. After working through *energy locks*, using hands only and sensing unblocking and restoration of energy, I'd end up deeply relaxed with cramping pain being the farthest thing from my mind.

While both Shiatsu and Jin Shin Jyutsu worked best in temporarily relieving cramps, the sessions were pricey and far exceeded my menstrual budget. To offset the cost of monthly visits, I'd perform *holds* said to help pelvic disorders on myself. Sitting on a chair with one foot on the floor and the other leg crossed over my knee, I'd hold what's called the *first aid* point located underneath

---

[46] "About Jin Shin Jyutsu." UC San Diego School of Medicine. Center for Integrative Medicine, 2018, www.medschool.ucsd.edu/som/fmph/research/cim/clinicalcare/Pages/jinshinjyutsu.aspx.

the ankle bone with one hand and my shin with the other for ten to twenty minutes.

Sometimes menstrual pain lessened and oftentimes the holds made cramps worse. Therefore, I'd perform deep breathing exercises instead. Calling upon techniques learned in movement, dance, and Tai Chi classes taken in college, I'd inhale deeply and slowly exhale, repetitiously, which somewhat helped in easing cramps.

In addition to Tui Na, Shiatsu, Jin Shin Jyutsu, self-message, and deep breathing exercises, I experimented with acupuncture, meditation and Thai Massage to alleviate cramps. However, all the massages, fine needles, and meditation in the world couldn't keep brutal menstrual cramps at bay. While CAM approaches may do wonders for some women with painful menstruation, those I explored only provided temporary relief. And, after an hour or so, incapacitating cramps would return.

With, seemingly, everything failing to relieve cramps, long-term, I re-evaluated my vegan lifestyle and vitamin supplement intake. Assuming the reasons why I continually struggled with painful periods was due to deficiencies in Omega-3 fatty acids which *"...are a key family of polyunsaturated fats"* that *"provide the starting point for making hormones that regulate blood clotting, contraction and relaxation of artery walls, and inflammation"*[47], I reverted to a non-vegan diet much to my boyfriend's chagrin.

In so doing, I began eating food rich in Omega-3 fatty acids such as tuna, herring, salmon, and halibut. I also incorporated rich sources of protein including lean meats, poultry, eggs, and soybeans. Due to lactose intolerance, I drank soymilk. However, later learning soy can exacerbate menstrual cramps, I eliminated soymilk, soybeans, tofu, and all other soy products.[48]

As recommended by a colleague in her late 50s, who battled painful menstruation for several years, I experimented with carbonated soda. Undergoing hysterectomy, at age 45, because she could no longer tolerate severe cramps and other menstrual-related problems, she swore up and down that carbonated drinks were highly effective in calming her cramps, before surgery.

---

[47] "Omega-3 Fatty Acids: An Essential Contribution." Harvard T.H. Chan School of Public Health, 2018, www.hsph.harvard.edu/nutritionsource/what-should-you-eat/fats-and-cholesterol/types-of-fat/omega-3-fats/.

[48] Nagata, C., Hirokawa, K., et al. "Associations of Menstrual Pain with Intakes of Soy, Fat and Dietary Fiber in Japanese Women." *Eur J Clin Nutr*. Jan. 2005, Vol. 59, no. 1, pp. 88-92, doi.org/10.1038/sj.ejcn.1602042, Abstract.

Therefore, I made a mad dash to the nearest supermarket and bought a case of soda shortly after our conversation.

In following her advice, I drank two cans per day for a month. However, when my next cycle began, pain seemed worse than the previous month. I also ended up with acne breakouts I hadn't experienced since my early teens.

Suggesting I also take antacids before onset of my periods and throughout the length of each cycle, left me baffled. Surely, I struggled with the idea of consuming a heartburn remedy for cramps. But, considering I was caught between a rock and a hard place, I adhered to her advice for approximately two cycles. And, like all other remedies, antacids weren't effective in reducing my menstrual cramps.

Since everything under the sun including beet juice, pickle juice, lemon juice, carrot juice, vinegar, molasses, and several other remedies couldn't tame my nerve-wracking menstrual cramps, I continued taking *non-steroidal anti-inflammatory drugs or NSAIDs*. Asserting to block *"…the production of prostaglandins, or chemicals believed to be associated with pain and inflammation"*[49], I took two 600 milligrams of ibuprofen every four hours, prior to and during my periods.

Regardless of how many NSAIDs I consumed over the course of each cycle, I still experienced pain which felt like a hula hoop spiked with ten-inch nails was twirling around my abdomen, pelvis and back. Fed up with prescription medication that seemed as potent as breath mints, I asked my gynecologist for morphine injections as suggested by a friend who had also struggled with agonizing menstrual cramps.

Gazing at me as if ten heads were protruding from my neck, he responded with something similar to, *"No. I don't prescribe morphine shots or other narcotics for menstrual pain, as they can be addictive."* Even though I shared research I conducted on morphine shots and addiction which states, *"...people who have continuing pain should not let the fear of dependence keep them from using narcotics to relieve their pain. Mental dependence*

---

[49] Hertz, S. "The Benefits and Risks of Pain Relievers: Q & A on NSAIDs with Sharon Hertz, M.D." 26 Sep. 2018. Food and Drug Administration, www.fda.gov/ForConsumers/ConsumerUpdates/ucm107856.htm.

(addiction) is not likely to occur when narcotics are used for this purpose."[50], according to an article published by Mayo Clinic, he still rejected my request and insisted that I continue taking ibuprofen.

My friend then recommended I see a female gynecologist who'd likely be more sympathetic and willing to administer morphine injections than male gynecologists. She also suggested I tell a series of lies to increase my chances of acquiring them.

As I brandished one lie after the next including *"NSAIDs cause allergic reactions and the many times I landed in the emergency room because of excruciating cramps, I was given morphine shots which helped significantly."*, she didn't show a smidgen of compassion. When asked to further explain my allergic reactions and provide the date of my last morphine shot, I was tongue-tied.

She, then, asked which type of pain medication I was currently taking. As soon as I mentioned that I was consuming two

---

[50] "Morphine (Injection Route)." Mayo Foundation for Medical Education and Research. 1 Oct. 2018. *Mayo Clinic*, www.mayoclinic.org/drugs-supplelments/morphine-injection-route/description/drg-20074202.

600 milligrams of ibuprofen every four hours, she said something like, *"I recommend that you continue taking them, as they should be able to control your menstrual cramps."* Escorting me to the front office, she wrote a prescription for more ibuprofen and I left without a morphine shot.

With mission unaccomplished and feeling like the world's worst liar, all I could think about was getting my hand on *speed* to put an end to my misery. Without any experience using the drug, other than knowing a few college friends who raved about the stimulant stopping menstrual cramps and menstrual cycles too, I wanted to give methamphetamine a shot out of sheer desperation. However, fear sat in as I reminisced about a disturbing experience I once had while attending college.

During break between classes, I visited a friend's art studio on campus. A brilliant painter whose creativity likely stemmed from the assortment of recreational drugs he took, regularly, I sat admiring his latest paintings as we chitchatted. In mentioning I had a *stomach ache*, even though my entire pelvic region felt like it was entangled in barbed wire, he reached into his artistically painted desk drawer and pulled out a plastic bag.

Emptying its contents onto a paper towel, he asked if I wanted to try *shrooms* to take my mind off stomach pain. Before I could say, *"Thanks, but no thanks."*, he began chomping on what looked like miniature mushroom covered in dirt. And, shortly after ingesting the fungi, he said I looked as if I were being replicated a hundred times with a hue of purple lights dancing around my body, which was certainly a cue for me to leave. Although we were friends, acting as sober sitter while he embarked on a trip to God knows where, just wasn't my cup of tea.

Waylaid by piercing cramps as I headed to my next class, I couldn't help but wonder what sort of issues he must've had to eat magic mushrooms, especially during school hours. Watching him hallucinate was so shocking, I promised myself I'd never do drugs. I even stopped eating *regular* mushrooms several years thereafter, fearing I'd hallucinate.

While prescription narcotics may not be suitable for treatment of painful menstruation, non-steroidal anti-inflammatory drugs and contraceptives proved useless. Forced to find effective treatment on my own, I continued experimenting with countless potions, lotions and other remedies claiming to control menstrual cramps. I even ate cactus, celery, and crushed Caraway seeds ballyhooing relief. However, they too were just as ineffective in numbing pain long enough for me to breathe.

Throwing a monkey wrench into my teenage and adult life and negatively affecting every aspect of it, cataclysmic crippling cramps ruled. I would cringe every time I glanced at my period calendar to view the start date of the next one. Anticipating sadistic cramps which felt like hosts of King crab trapped inside my uterus and hell-bent on clawing their way to freedom, became a way of life.

CHAPTER 2
What Woes of the Womb!

Plagued by PMS and PMDD

With menstrual cramps and an entourage of atrocious *premenstrual syndrome (PMS)* symptoms infiltrating my body and psyche as early as at age 16, had I possessed telekinetic power like the main character in the film *Carrie*[51], I would have yanked my womb out, bashed it with a bat, and buried the damned thing beneath the earth.

PMS attacked with such vengeance, I must've had 149 of over 150 known physical, emotional and behavioral symptoms.[52] Physically, I endured abdominal and pelvic pain, bloating, headache, fatigue, nausea, weight gain, and several other symptoms.

Emotionally and behaviorally, I experienced anxiety, moodiness, insomnia, irritability, and an array of other *cruel* symptoms. Surfacing, approximately, a week before onset of my periods, like clockwork, I'd go into *fight* mode. A single push of my

---

[51] *Carrie*, written by Stephen King, directed by Brian De Palma, United Artists, 1976.
[52] "Premenstrual Syndrome (PMS) and Premenstrual Dysphoric Disorder (PMDD)." 31 Aug. 2018. Center for *Young Women's Health*, www.youngwomenshealth.org/2013/10/31/pms/#.

button would cause me to transform into a belligerent witch consumed with an itching need to unleash fury upon those who would, unintentionally, cause my normal emotional equilibrium to tailspin.

Oftentimes, the red-eyed demon in me would berate those who failed to see things my way. The most trivial matter would become catastrophic. And, any attempt at appeasing me while in the clutches PMS was usually met with anger of astronomical proportions. Surely, recipients of my out-of-character outbursts must've thought I had multiple personality disorder, bipolar disorder, or both.

Then, a day or two prior to the bursting of blood's floodgates, I'd go into *flight* mode. Likely triggered by the onset of excruciating abdominal and pelvic pain, I'd become edgy and hypersensitive. Mere conversations would cause tsunami-like tears and disagreements would trigger uncontrollable crying fits.

I'd blame others for being insensitive during my PMS meltdowns, even though most hadn't a clue as to what I was going through. Thereafter, I'd *flee the scene* and cease all communication to avoid further distress. But, as soon as menstruation began, I wanted nothing more than to fling myself into a deep, dark ditch after realizing my emotions were out of control and I had likely caused others trauma.

Shockingly, I've never harmed anyone while in the grips of PMS. Although tempted to lay one across the mouths of those who brought out the worst in me during the beginning phase of PMS, I'd instead express my distaste using verbal vulgarities. I would snap at checkout clerks who'd place a gazillion items in a single bag; become unglued while standing in slow-moving lines; and incite arguments in relationships too.

Speaking of relationships, I dated a wonderful guy while attending college. In witnessing my turbulent, cyclical behavior during the first few months, I'm surprised he didn't hit the road and run for his life. Verbally clobbering him for unjustifiable reasons, I'd find fault with practically everything he'd say and do. And, in seeking vengeance for his *wrongdoings*, I'd recite over and over how I wished I had never met him.

Able to sense when the wrath of PMS was upon me, over time, he'd try his best to brace himself as I morphed into his worst nightmare, ranting about everything under the sun and regurgitating past quarrels I couldn't seem to let go of.

Doing everything in his power to ensure my days of premenstrual affliction were as comfortable as possible, he'd prepare my favorite herbal teas, rub my stomach, massage my hands and feet, and whisper sweet nothings in my ear. However, bearing the brunt of my overwhelming mood swings and spitfire hissy fits, often resulted in him storming out of the house, car, restaurants, and all else. In turn, I'd break up with him almost every month for doing so.

I remember dragging him through hormonal hell one early evening. Picking me up from work, as usual, I discussed every detail of my awful day. As if he were a soundboard, I complained about staff I supervised and customers who drove me crazy. I also grumbled about the toilet leak that flooded the ladies' restroom, causing myself and staff to use the restrooms at a nearby coffee shop; and the broken air conditioner that felt like I'd spent eight hours in a sweat shop. Agitated and overwhelmed, due to my PMS state of being, I contemplated walking off the job several times that day.

While strolling, hand in hand, to our favorite Vietnamese

restaurant a few blocks away, I could tell he was excited about something as he kept staring at me and smiling. Walking a few steps ahead of me he, suddenly, dropped to one knee. In asking, *"What on earth are you doing on the ground?"*, he reached into his pocket and pulled out a royal blue velvet box. Flicking it open in the palm of his hand, I stood stunned while glaring at the cheapest-looking, engagement ring I had ever seen.

As my blood began boiling, he placed what must've had ten, miniscule ruby and diamond chips on my finger. Unable to hide my emotions since PMS wouldn't let me, I lashed out and said, *"Is this your idea of an engagement ring? I'm your woman, not your teenage sweetheart. So, take it back to the five and dime you, obviously, bought it from!"*

Standing to his feet astonished, I asked, *"If you love me as much as you say you do, why would you give me a ring that looks like something sifted out of a Cracker Jack box?"* At this point, he looked as if he had seen an apparition. Incensed by my reaction, he reneged on dining out and suggested we head home. Within the next few days, the clouds of PMS had passed over and my period began. As I returned to my normal self, I was back in love with him—dirt-cheap ring and all.

Inevitably, PMS destroyed our relationship of five years. After verbally assassinating him during a PMS laden argument, I ended the relationship, packed my bags, and moved over a hundred miles away. Running him ragged with my monthly explosions which left him puzzled, powerless and pissed off, I wanted nothing more than for him to find someone either PMS-free or with fewer horrendous symptoms than my own.

PMS also caused countless catastrophes in which friends, family and even strangers were unluckily entangled. One such incident occurred on Christmas Eve when a woman stepped in front of me as I stood in line to buy last minute gifts. Normally, I would have said, *"Excuse me ma'am, but the end of the line is back there."*, assuming she was unaware of jumping the line. However, the crudeness of PMS caused me to lose all rationale as I uttered something like, *"Miss, are you blind? Can't you see there's a line spiraling to the back of the store?"*

Wielding a revolting look with no intentions of moving, I began shouting vulgarities at the top of my lungs. Although enraged to the point of wanting to beat the woman's brains out, I kept repeating, *"Lady, you better move now!"*, until she stepped out of the line.

While ringing me up, the checkout clerk called security over the intercom. Quickly gathering my bags and exiting the store before security arrived, I thanked my lucky stars I didn't succumb to the impulses of PMS. Being angry for hours, thereafter, certainly made gift wrapping uneventful that evening. However, it was far better than being behind bars.

When my period arrived a few days later, I knew the fiasco at the store was entirely PMS-fueled. Embarrassed by my volatile behavior and upset that I couldn't control it, I began referring to PMS as Place in Major Sanatorium, Psychotic Mean Streak, Potential Maiming Suspect, and Psychiatrist Meant Schizophrenic, hoping to find some solace.

When a vile form of PMS called *premenstrual dysphoric disorder (PMDD)* emerged during my mid-20s, adding a severe set of emotional, physical and behavioral symptoms to my plate of premenstrual hell, I wanted to call life quits.

Such new symptoms included sudden mood changes, heightened sensitivity, feeling overwhelmed and out of control, social withdrawal, abdominal spasms, constipation, frequent urination, food and ice cravings, swollen hands and feet, and breast tenderness and engorgement. And, symptoms I was already battling magnified a hundredfold, seemingly.

Having well over five of the eleven or so symptoms required for a PMDD diagnosis, all hell would break loose days before my periods. One such forgettable PMDD-related incident occurred while attending a weekend-long family reunion at the World Trade Center in New York City—a few years before 911.

Arriving from California in the late evening, I visited my sister and her daughter in their hotel room before heading to my parent's room. While chitchatting for a few hours, abdominal spasms struck which signified my period was twenty-four to forty-eight hours away. Feeling miserable, tired and uncomfortable sitting on the chair, I asked my sister if I could sleep on the full-size bed with my thirteen-year-old niece.

Her response which was similar to, *"Sorry, but my daughter sleeps rather wild and needs plenty of room to stretch out."* mortified me. While she had every right to ensure her daughter had ample space to rest comfortably, my PMDD-filled filter highly disagreed.

In my head, it was the worst thing a human being could do to another—especially to a family member. With hypersensitivity gone amuck and unwilling to disturb my parents wee hours in the night, I curled into the fetal position on the floor and silently cried myself to sleep.

Waking with a face of dried tears and bloodshot eyes that morning, I went to my parent's hotel room and tearfully explained what had happened. Although they did everything to console me, I couldn't stop crying. Had they known about my disorder, perhaps they would have understood why I was uncontrollably emotional. And, upon arrival of my period, a day or two later, I was so ashamed that I ceased communication with my sister for over two years.

Another PMDD-related catastrophe occurred on my birthday. In celebration, my boyfriend at the time, decided to bake a cake. Therefore, we went to the grocery store to buy ingredients. As we headed toward the checkout line, a woman and her newborn strolled past us. Abruptly turning his head around as if his neck had snapped, I followed suit. In seeing him stare at the woman's derriere, I instantly became unglued and burst into a tirade.

While driving home, I expressed how disrespectful it was of him to gaze at another woman in my presence. Responding with something like, *"I was just admiring the newborn, that's all."* made me even more livid considering the baby was in a covered stroller. And, when we arrived home, my expletives were so brazen, I'm surprised he didn't run for the hills. Instead, he stood beating cake batter and avoiding eye contact.

When done, cooled and frosted with chocolate, an hour or so later, I lifted the cake off the counter and threw it on the floor. In my PMDD mind, that was where it belonged. Surely, he should have known the worst thing a man could do when walking arm in arm with a woman with PMDD, is look at another. It's a *recipe* for disaster.

PMDD also disrupted my work life, causing my normal interpersonal functioning to fly out the window. Overanalyzing and overreacting to practically everything, I would either convince myself certain colleagues were out to ruin my stellar work ethic, or I was being taken advantage of whenever my workload increased. Other times, emotions would flare just because co-workers failed to respond to my *"Good Morning"* greetings.

Additionally, receiving constructive criticism at work was so traumatic, I would run to the restroom and break down in tears. While I never used the disorder as a free pass to flip out and harangue others, my PMDD reactions clearly warranted both emotional awareness and anger management classes.

I remember a manager once asking something similar to, *"I really like what you've done, however, can you create a more stylized template for this particular training manual?"* With PMDD symptoms lingering in the wings, I interpreted her request as poor job performance and that my employment was in jeopardy. As I burst into tears, she not only tried to comfort me, she begged that I share what she had done wrong.

From that embarrassing point forward, I did all I could to control emotional symptoms of PMDD, especially when they'd surface while at work. I'd view my menstrual calendar, regularly, which helped in anticipating when mood swings were likely to erupt. I avoided interactions that would trigger either hyper-sensitivity or aggression. And, I refrained from making important, work-related and life decisions until symptoms subsided.

Regardless, the disorder progressively worsened which

necessitated intervention by health care providers. In furnishing a laundry list of persistent PMDD complaints ranging from anxiety to extreme moodiness; providing a copy of my menstrual diary, detailing when symptoms were mild, moderate, or severe each month; and divulging remedies I used in attempt to combat them, I'd receive the usual, *'What you're experiencing are normal symptoms that occur before menstruation in many women. Continue taking birth control pills to reduce these symptoms.'* response.

In my late 20s, a doctor recommended antidepressant. Knowing little about this class of drugs, I assumed I'd have to take them for the rest of my life, see a psychiatrist on a regular basis and, perhaps pay a visit to the nearest psych ward. Likewise, I was afraid antidepressants would alter my personality, become addictive, and cause adverse side effects since I was taking high-dose pain medication for menstrual cramps.

Apparently, visiting the doctor's office while experiencing PMDD symptoms was a bad idea. Having a glimpse as to what PMMD looks and sounds like, I tearfully explained how frustrated I was with my insufferable cycles. After recounting every aspect of my usual premenstrual plight, he suggested I stop taking birth control pills and start taking antidepressants.

Referred to as *selective serotonin re-uptake inhibitors* or *SSRIs*, antidepressants *"...ease depression by increasing levels of serotonin in the brain."*[53] According to Mayo Clinic, *"serotonin is one of the chemical messengers (neurotransmitters) that carry signals between brain cells. SSRIs block the reabsorption (reuptake) of serotonin in the brain, making more serotonin available."*[54]

Learning that SSRIs are commonly used to treat moderate to severe depression made me apprehensive about taking them. Since I wasn't clinically depressed—just highly pissed off a few days each month because of my periods, I couldn't justify taking them. However, knowing I couldn't manage PMDD symptoms on my own and receiving my doctor's assurance that SSRIs will reduce or eliminate emotional symptoms of PMDD, I gave paroxetine a try on an intermittent basis.

---

[53] "Selective Serotonin Reuptake Inhibitors (SSRIs)." 17 May 2018. *Mayo Clinic*, www.mayoclinic.org/diseases-conditions/depression/in-depth/ssris/art-20044825.
[54] "Selective Serotonin Reuptake Inhibitors (SSRIs)." 17 May 2018. *Mayo Clinic*, www.mayoclinic.org/diseases-conditions/depression/in-depth/ssris/art-20044825.

Known as *luteal-phase dosing*[55], I only had to take the antidepressant after ovulation and before menstruation began, as opposed to every day. And, over the next three cycles or so, emotional and behavioral symptoms were less noticeable days prior to my periods. In fact, my positive response to the SSRI was on par with a study which states, *"... 60% to 90% of women with PMDD respond to treatment with drugs that block reuptake of serotonin..."*[56]

Even though paroxetine proved beneficial in decreasing most emotional and behavioral symptoms of PMDD, it caused side effects that would make a blue whale to keel over. A few hours after taking them, I felt like a zombie and experienced headaches equivalent to being bashed in the head with a two by four as well as nausea, drowsiness, dry mouth, and diarrhea.

Apparently, my doctor mistook me for a marine mammal in prescribing the antidepressant. Considering symptoms only

---

[55] Halbreich, U. and Kahn LS. "Treatment of Premenstrual Dysphoric Disorder with Luteal Phase Dosing of Sertraline." *Expert Opin Pharmacother*, Nov. 2003, Vol. 4, no. 11, pp. 2065-2078, doi:10.1517/14656566.4.11.2065, Abstract.

[56] "Treating Premenstrual Dysphoric Disorder." Harvard Health Publications. Oct. 2009. *Harvard Medical School*, www.health.harvard.edu/womens-health/treating-premenstrual-dysphoric-disorder.

appeared during the premenstrual phase of my cycles, I was unwilling to tolerate side effects which seemed worse than the symptoms I endured. Instead, I tried the dietary supplement S-adenosyl-L-methionine (SAM-e), *"a chemical that is found naturally in the body."*[57] However, I couldn't bear the side effects of nausea and stomach upset after taking the recommended 800 milligram capsule per day, for approximately three months. Therefore, I halted use of SAM-e.

I, then, experimented with evening primrose oil supplements that contain the fatty acid gamma-linolenic acid (GLA) and claim to treat certain PMDD symptoms.[58] Knowing women who raved about evening primrose oil, I took eight 500 milligram capsules per day well over six months. However, my symptoms remained unchanged.

Regularly frequenting vitamin and health food stores in hopes of finding supplements to relieve PMDD symptoms, I'd ask

---

[57] "S-Adenosyl-L-Methionine (SAMe): In Depth." National Center for Complementary and Integrative Health. Jan. 2017. *National Institutes of Health*, www.nccih.nih.gov/health/supplements/SAMe.

[58] "Evening Primrose Oil." National Center for Complementary and Integrative Health. Sep. 2016. *National Institutes of Health*, www.nccih.nih.gov/health/eveningprimrose.

store clerks, *"What do you recommend for PMDD?"* While most had never heard of the disorder, those familiar with PMS, at least, usually suggested St. John's wort *"...for "the blues" or depression and symptoms that sometimes go along with mood such as nervousness, tiredness, poor appetite, and trouble sleeping."*[59]

In fact, a case report published in the International Journal of Psychiatry Medicine propose, *"...St. John's wort could be an alternative medication for PMDD, especially for patients experiencing intolerable side effects with selective serotonin reuptake inhibitors."*[60] The report is based on a case in which a patient was given 900 milligrams of St. John's wort per day. And, the results revealed notable improvement of PMMD symptoms after a five-month follow up. However, in my case, symptoms remained unchanged after consuming 300 milligrams of St. John's wort three times a day, for approximately four months.

Frustrated with herbal supplements touting to treat PMDD, I

---

[59] "St. John's Wort." 2018. *WebMD*, www.webmd.com/vitamins/ai/ingredientmono-329/st-johns-wort.

[60] Huang, K-L. and Tsai, S-J. "St. John's Wort (Hypericum Perforatum) as a Treatment for Premenstrual Dysphoric Disorder: Case Report." *Int J Psychiatry Med*, 1 Sep. 2003, Vol. 33, no. 3, pp. 295-297, doi.org/10.2190/RERY-N6AC-NADC-EHY4, Abstract.

made a number of dietary changes hoping to minimize my symptoms. Instead of eating one or two large meals a day, I ate three to four smaller ones, ensuring each contained essential nutrients, low carbohydrates, and healthy fats. Additionally, I replaced white bread, pasta, and sugary cereals with high-fiber, complex carbohydrates such as whole grain bread, whole wheat pasta, and sugar-free cereals.

I eliminated canned, bagged, and boxed food containing high sodium as they would exacerbate premenstrual headaches. I tapered my intake of coffee and tea since caffeine increased anxiety and gave me the *shakes* too. Likewise, I limited alcohol consumption considering the least amount caused fatigue, especially during the premenstrual phase of my cycles.

Exercising while stricken with a multitude of PMDD symptoms was the last thing on my mind. Though I'd push myself to walk short intervals at a slow pace and perform other low impact exercises to reduce symptoms to tolerable levels, I still experienced PMDD-related turmoil most months. Like a pendulum, my mood swings would sway from anger to tearfulness in a New York minute, seemingly. However, onset of my periods would make most symptoms *go poof.*

Upon return to normalcy, I'd reminisce about my premenstrual showdowns which customarily caused others distress. My inner voice would say, *"You must find better ways of keeping your emotions in check days prior to your periods!"* as I tried taking responsibility for my behavior by apologizing for my outbursts. But, before the dust could settle, unrelenting symptoms would summon me all over again—the next month.

Neither *imagined* nor *all in my head*, symptoms of PMS and PMDD are real. In fact, *"Symptoms of PMS have been reported to affect as many as 90% of women of reproductive age sometime during their lives.'*[61], in the United States. And, according to researchers at National Institutes of Health (NIH), PMDD *"…affects 2 to 5 percent of women of reproductive age."*

Encouragingly, recent research shows a link between a suspect gene's response to estrogen and progesterone in women with PMDD and certain symptoms of the disorder some women

---

[61] Moreno, MA., Zuckerman AL., et al. "Premenstrual Syndrome." *Medscape*, 1 Sep. 2016, www.emedicine.medscape.com/article/953696-overview.

experience.[62] Though further investigation is required, a press release published by the National Institute of Mental Health in 2017 states, *"National Institutes of Health (NIH) researchers have discovered molecular mechanisms that may underlie a woman's susceptibility to disabling irritability, sadness, and anxiety in the days leading up to her menstrual period."*[63]

While some health care providers did their due diligence in attempting to treat my PMS and PMDD symptoms, respectfully, they failed to order tests, like ultrasound, to rule out any underlying condition which may have exacerbated these disorders with causes that are yet to be determined. Therefore, I suffered from adolescence to my late 30s.

With premenstrual symptoms diminishing my quality of life; affecting regular activities such as school, college and work; destroying my social life; damaging relationships; and inhibiting my

---

[62] Dubey, N., Hoffman, JF., et al. "The ESC/E(Z) Complex, An Effector of Response to Ovarian Steroids, Manifests an Intrinsic Difference in Cells from Women with Premenstrual Dysphoric Disorder." *Molecular Psychiatry*, Aug. 2017, Vol. 22, pp. 1172-1184, doi:10.1038/mp.2016.229.

[63] "Sex Hormone–Sensitive Gene Complex Linked to Premenstrual Mood Disorder." National Institute of Mental Health. 3 Jan. 2017. *National Institutes of Health*, www.nimh.nih.gov/news/science-news/2017/sex-hormone-sensitive-gene-complex-linked-to-premenstrual-mood-disorder.shtml, Press Release.

ability to focus and concentrate on anything other than finding ways to cope with the disorders, I'm surprised I didn't jump off a skyscraper to end it all.

Instead, I continued taking ineffective pain medication and birth control pills. And, I monitored patterns of my symptoms by documenting dates and times they'd occur, and emotional, behavior and physical outcomes after taking medications, birth control pills as well as other remedies I experimented with. Doing so helped me gauge when premenstrual chaos was likely to occur, as I hoped and prayed for merciful menstruation each month.

Belly Bloating Bouts

By age 28, I looked as if I were several months pregnant a few days prior to and during my periods. Driven to the brink of insanity when asked, *"Is it a boy or girl?"* or *"How far along are you?"*, I'd copiously swear I wasn't with child. And, whenever asked to explain why my belly was swelly, I'd often brandish white lies such as, *"I ate like a glutinous pig last night.", or "The office vending machine keeps calling my name."*

Battling abdominal bloating for nearly 15 years, one may have thought I was devouring meat and potatoes for breakfast, lunch, and dinner. My face would appear as puffy as a plump throw pillow. My breasts would become so engorged, they looked as if they were about to detonate. And, my usual medium-width feet would swell to the point of requiring wide-width shoes.

Although I ate moderately and oftentimes experienced loss of appetite, I still gained an upward of ten pounds during most cycles. Usually a size ten in clothing, I'd balloon to size twelve. To accommodate my expanding stomach, I wore over-sized blouses and dresses resembling moo-moos. With such loose-fitting attire inciting stares and comments, I began wearing my normal clothing with either girdles or other tummy control garments underneath, especially when in public.

In fact, I remember trying on every suit in my closet the night before a job interview. Considering I was in the premenstrual phase of my cycle, my bulging belly and bourgeoning breasts made it impossible to zip skirts and button jackets. But, after cramming into a full-body shaper that seemed to flatten everything except my neck, I was able to fit into one of my suits.

While bloated and barely breathing throughout the forty-five-minute interview, I presented samples of my instructional design and technical writing material. Then, I answered what seemed like a hundred questions that were posed by the panel of four. When the interview was over, I placed the materials in my briefcase and stood.

As I reached across the table to shake hands with one of the panelists, my skirt zipper broke—as did the hook and eye. Swinging my handbag behind me to shield my wardrobe malfunction, I shook hands with the others then jetted out of the conference room as fast as a falcon.

Trailing behind to escort me to the elevator, I feared all eyes were glued to my derriere encased in the white body shaper I had worn. When they boarded too, I thought I was going to die. Standing propped against the back wall, as still as a statue, as they discussed how impressed they were with the samples I had shown, I prayed for a power outage.

After taking what seemed like the longest elevator ride ever, I was told to have a seat in reception area and wait for the receptionist to validate my parking ticket. Instead, I pretended to search my handbag for my car key just to remain standing. Had I sat down, I may have ended up bottomless.

Thankfully, the receptionist returned within a few minutes and handed me a parking sticker. Holding my skirt up with one hand while clutching my briefcase and handbag with the other, I asked her to point me in the direction of the restroom. Once inside, I used bobby pins and paper clips to temporarily repair my skirt. Then, I waddled out of the building like a duck, believing my premenstrual bloating problem couldn't get any worse.

I was proven wrong when a friend suggested I go on a blind date with a man whom she thought would be a perfect match for me. Initially, I was excited about getting back into the dating scene.

But, after consulting my menstrual diary and seeing that bloating days were at hand, naturally, I had second thoughts in accepting his lunch invitation the next day. Later deciding I wasn't going to let my premenstrual woes including social withdrawal dampen my life as they had for years, I spent the entire evening rummaging through my closet to find casual attire that would hide my rotund tummy yet make me look appealing.

Skipping dinner the night before with hopes of minimizing abdominal protrusion, I arrived at the restaurant famished. After a few minutes of seeing stars as I perused the menu, I quickly selected the first platter image. Normally, I'd order a salad on a first date so I could focus more on chemistry than food. However, my hunger pains favored steak and potatoes, so I ordered just that.

As we dined and engaged in getting-to-know conversation for an hour or so, I could feel my stomach expand beyond the waist perimeter of my form-fitting jeans. Leaning back in the chair helped ease some discomfort likely due to the combination of premenstrual bloating, talking while chewing, and devouring my food quicker than I should have. However, when throbbing sensations in my lower abdomen struck, moments later, I excused myself and headed to the restroom.

While struggling to unzip my jeans so I could breathe, out pops my swollen abdomen that looked as if I had a six-month bun in the oven. With welt lines encircling it, I stood at the sink patting them lightly with a wet paper towel to calm the stinging. Since zipping my jeans was impossible, I returned to my date with my blouse hanging on the outside and covering my blossoming belly underneath it.

Experiencing abdominal bloating while at work was just as unsettling. Even though I kept close tabs on bloating days by viewing my menstrual diary, there was no telling how large my abdomen would expand. To preempt buttons from popping off and zippers from breaking, oftentimes, I'd partially unzip my pants or skirt to accommodate my jutting belly while sitting behind my desk or conference room table.

I remember eating a relatively light lunch—a salad, chips, and apple juice at my desk, one premenstrual day. An hour or so later, my abdomen was as plump as a rump roast. As I discreetly unbuttoned and unzipped my pants to breathe, ear-piecing alarms rang so loud the entire world probably knew my company was having a fire drill.

Grabbing my handbag, I headed to the stairwell and walked down several flights alongside other employees. Forgetting my pants were undone, I placed my thumb through a belt hoop to prevent them from falling below my hips. And, once outside, I stood amongst hundreds holding onto the hoop for dear life.

After twenty minutes elapsed with no telling when we could head back into the building, I had to find a way to fasten my pants and relax my pulsating thumb. Moving as far away from the crowd as I could and ending up inside the enclosure gates of a dumpster, I reached inside my purse that contained everything but the kitchen sink—to find safety pins.

Searching high and low to no avail, I grabbed hold of waxed dental floss and looked at it in a way I had never before. Dispensing every inch out of its casing, I threaded the hoops twice around and tied a knot. With my jacket covering my *flossed* waist, I rejoined my colleagues feeling confident my pants were securely fastened and smelling minty. Certainly, the experience taught me to carry safety pins, a needle and thread, and belt at all times.

To minimize premenstrual bloating embarrassment, I

reorganized both my wardrobe and dresser drawers. The right side contained clothes that were a size larger and comfortable to wear when bloated. And, my regular-sized clothes were kept on the left. Had I not arranged them in this manner, I would have risked being charged with indecent exposure in the workplace.

Sleeping with a hard, bloated abdomen was equally nerve-wracking. Since it felt as if a basketball was lodged in my gut, I usually slept on my back. I would even lay two, king-size pillows on both sides of my body to prevent turning over. But, regardless of my sleep position habits, abdominal swelling remained a constant battle.

Overwhelmed with the cyclic bloating bug, I had a *whale* of a time twisting, turning, and waking up several times, particularly at night. In attempt to combat *"menstrual insomnia"*[64], I'd customarily eat a slice of bread or a few crackers then take a pain pill or two. While waiting for the discomforting sense of fullness and pressure to ease, I'd stare at my big bloated belly thinking, *"What*

---

[64] Laliberte, M. "13 Ways to Deal with Menstrual Insomnia: Tossing and Turning Before your Period? You're Not Alone." 23 Jan. 2017. *Reader's Digest*, www.rd.com/health/wellness/menstrual-insomnia.

on earth could possibly be growing inside me?", especially when it appeared larger than the last time I glanced at it. Then, eventually, I'd fall asleep.

Unable to control my expectant-looking abdomen was a heavy blow to my self-esteem. Abdominal bloating also destroyed my dating life. Assuming I was *knocked up*, most men wouldn't even approach me. And, trying to convince neighbors and friends that I wasn't pregnant became so daunting, I didn't want to leave the house.

Before seeking medical help, I read several books and journals on abdominal bloating, menstrual bloating, continuous abdominal distension as well as swollen belly, hoping to find information on why I constantly bloated prior to and during my periods. Albeit useful, I only found general information similar to an abstract published in the Harvard Review of Psychiatry which states, *"Somatic complaints, including breast tenderness and bloating, also can prove disruptive to women's overall functioning and quality of life. Recent evidence suggests that individual sensitivity to cyclical variations in levels of gonadal hormones may predispose certain women to experience these mood, behavioral, and somatic symptoms. Treatments include: antidepressants of the serotonin reuptake inhibitor class, taken intermittently or throughout the menstrual cycle; medications that suppress ovarian cyclicity; and newer oral contraceptives with novel progestins.'*[65]

Preferring to take the self-help route first, I adjusted my diet by eliminating what may have worsened abdominal bloating. I replaced gas-producing food such as dairy, cabbage, broccoli, cauliflower, and beans with high fiber food including unprocessed wheat bran, whole grains, and dried fruit. I also incorporated herbal remedies purporting to reduce abdominal bloating and speed up digestion such as fennel, coriander and cumin seeds as well as ginger root.

I decreased my intake of fatty food since fat delays stomach emptying and food with high levels of starch, sugar, salt and refined carbohydrates that increases estrogen levels.[66] Additionally, I limited caffeine, alcohol and carbonated drinks since consuming

---

[65] Cunningham, J., Yonkers, KA., et al. "Update on Research and Treatment of Premenstrual Dysphoric Disorder." Apr. 2009, Vol. 17, no. 2, pp. 120-137. *Harv Rev Psychiatry*, doi:10.1080/10673220902891836, Abstract.

[66] Mushref, MA. and Srinivasan, S. "Effect of High Fat-Diet and Obesity on Gastrointestinal Motility." *Ann Transl Med,* 2013, Vol. 1, no. 2, p. 14, doi:10.3978/j.issn.2305-5839.2012.11.01, Abstract.

these liquids in large amounts can lead to bloating.[67] And, I ceased taking calcium and iron as both seemed to exacerbate bloating and cause gas too.

I also performed low-impact aerobic exercises, as often as possible, and applied self-massage techniques to help jumpstart the digestive process. However, all the massaging, exercising, and dietary adjustments in the world couldn't beat the bloat.

Since I could neither treat nor prevent my abdomen from expanding like yeast on my own, I sought the advice of health care providers. Suggesting I take diuretics also referred to as *water pills* to reduce abdominal bloating, distension, and fluid buildup, I took them over the course of three or four cycles. However, with little effect and later learning diuretics can cause kidney damage when taken in combination with ibuprofen or other non-steroidal anti-inflammatory drug[68], I stopped taking them.

Unable to minimize abdominal bloating and distension with

---

[67] Cozma-Petruţ, A., Loghin, F., et al. "Diet in Irritable Bowel Syndrome: What to Recommend, Not What to Forbid to Patients!" *World J Gastroenterol*, 2017, Vol. 23, no. 21, pp. 3771-3783, doi:10.3748/wjg.v23.i21.3771, Abstract.
[68] Hörl, WH. "Nonsteroidal Anti-Inflammatory Drugs and the Kidney." *Pharmaceuticals (Basel, Switzerland)*, Vol. 3, no. 7, pp. 2291-2321, 21 Jul. 2010, doi:10.3390/ph3072291, Abstract.

diuretics and other remedies I experimented with, I assumed constipation was the cause. In fact, I struggled with constipation, yet another symptom of PMS and PMDD, from age 28 to 43. Commonly occurring a week before my periods, rectal blockage and pressure felt as if pillars of rocks were residing inside my rectum.

To brace myself for hellish bowel movements, I would drink a half pint of prune juice and rub myself with either witch hazel wipes or mineral oil. With agonizing pain knocking the wind out of me, I'd sit leaning back on the tank while gripping onto the edge of the sink. Often reduced to tears from paralyzing pain, I'd pray for immediate defecation which often felt like I was excreting through a stitched bottom.

Attacked with constipation when away from home was just as torturous and humiliating. I remember battling a bad case of what I called *bloatstipation* throughout the day. By evening, I felt so miserable, I wanted to beat the *crap* out of my big belly with a baton. Instead, I attended a Fourth of July celebration at a neighbor's house. I felt compelled to join them as I had in past years and hopeful that being outdoors would take my mind off constipation.

Shortly after nibbling on a variety of food, I could hear my stomach gurgling as pain began radiating with such intensity, I couldn't move. As I pretended like I was having a grand ole time, I sat on a plastic patio chair squirming and groaning under my breath. By rocking from side to side and placing my weight on each cheek for several minutes, I was able to gain some relief.

As my neighbors began setting off fireworks, a fleeting thought of placing a lit M-80 where the sun doesn't shine to trigger a bowel movement, crossed my mind. With my stomach gurgling and rectum burning like a chimney, I told my neighbors I had to check up on my dog and would return. Instead, I ended up sitting on the toilet for over twenty minutes, howling like a coyote while waiting for my rectal storage room to open its doors. And, when that bitter sweet, *"Yay, I'm about to excrete!"* moment was nigh, it felt like firewood logs were being evacuated with a blow torch.

Stricken with infrequent bowel movements warranted trips to the emergency room. Bloated and unable to defecate for two weeks, I once drove myself to the ER. When finally seen after the agonizing two-hour wait, moaning stopped and bawling began as the physician performed a *digital rectal exam*, a routine screening test that can detect underlying conditions in both women and men such as bladder and rectum abnormalities and tumors of the prostate.[69] Since I had never undergone a rectal exam, I trembled on bended knee while trying to make sense as to why his gloved, lubricated finger was pushing in what needed to come out.

After examining me, administering intravenous fluids, and ordering a CT scan, he informed me that dry, hardened stool was packed so tight in my large intestine, normal pushing action of the colon wasn't enough to eject all the crap inside me. He, then, diagnosed me with chronic constipation, a condition common in the elderly, and gave me prescriptions for saline laxatives, rectal suppositories, and pain medication.

As luck would have it, I ended up in the emergency room a second time, while visiting my family in New York. Apparently, a combination of home-cooked meals, fast food, and premenstrual symptoms caused my colon to go into shock. Constipated for approximately a week, I was given magnesium hydroxide and pain

---

[69] "Digital Rectal Exam (DRE)." Cedars-Sinai. 2018. www.cedars-sinai.edu/Patients/Programs-and-Services/Urology-Academic-Practice/Conditions-and-Treatments/Diagnostic-Testing/Digital-Rectal-Exam-DRE.aspx.

medication—without being subjected to another dreadful rectal exam, thankfully. And, within an hour or so, I eliminated what felt like a months' worth of waste.

During discharge, the ER nurse recommended I drink eight glasses of water daily and lie off food high in carbohydrates and fat while vacationing. She also suggested I drink prune juice more often than I had been drinking and take a mild laxative once a week to prevent fecal impaction.

Since I hadn't been diagnosed with anything other than chronic constipation, at the time, I assumed I simply had to watch what I ate and take either saline laxatives, rectal suppositories or stool softeners to regulate my bowel movements. However, I still struggled with constipation.

Uncontrollable Urinary Urges

A few days before my periods, my bladder usually felt as if it were sitting on a bed of needles instead of my pelvic floor. Frequent urination, another wearying symptom of the womb, often left me as saturated as a newborn. In fact, the slightest chuckle, cough, or sneeze would cause my urinary dam to break loose with such force, sanitizing mattresses, mopping floors, and spot treating carpet became premenstrual household chores.

Letting go at the wrong times and in the wrong places was even more maddening, as everything in line of my urinary fire would fall victim. Car seats, chairs, and cement too. I remember taking a few sips from my water bottle as I drove to the park with my dog. As soon as we arrived, I felt bladder pressure so intense, I thought it had prolapsed. Even though the urge to urinate was strong, I figured I could hold it until I reached the restroom that was a few yards away. But, while walking at stop and go speed as my pooch greeted other dogs and urinated on seemingly every patch of grass we came upon, I let go like a racehorse on diuretics.

As I watched urine drench my light grey sweatpants and flow through crevices of asphalt beneath me, I was embarrassed to tears. Afraid others would notice my *wet state*, I hurriedly walked back to my car. Protecting the seat by yanking the waterproof cover from under my dog, who sat on the back seat dazed and confused about our short outing, I drove home feeling as if I were a canine that day.

While there were enumerable incidents in which my bladder felt as if it had ruptured, an unforgettable one occurred at the dentist's office. In dire need of a root canal although apprehensive about numbing needles and the whole nine yards, I requested an emergency appointment.

As I walked through the door, the overpowering smell of antiseptic and distant drilling sounds unglued me and my hair weave too. When the dental assistant called my name minutes later, surely, I contemplated hiding behind the tall, leafy floor plant so she'd assume I was a no-show. But, since my toothache was unbearable, I followed her to the exam room as hesitant as a squirrel.

Before sitting in the dental chair, I asked the assistant how long the procedure was going to take. Considering I was in the premenstrual phase of my period which caused me to urinate frequently, I needed to know. And, when told anywhere between thirty minutes to an hour, I darted to the restroom even though I didn't have an urge.

Upon returning, the dentist placed numbing gel on the inside of my cheek. Several minutes later, he began pulling it every which way to get at nerves I never knew were in my mouth. Then came the lidocaine shots that didn't feel, at all, like the "*light pricks*" he promised.

When as numb as a drunkard with my jaws jacked open, the assistant began suctioning, the dentist started drilling away, and I began raining urine. To get the assistant's attention, I squeezed her hand so hard I'm surprised I didn't burst a blood vessel. Instantly, the dentist turned the screeching drill off and looked at me perplexed.

Without saying a word, I *slid* off the chair and raced to the restroom. When I returned, they seemed clueless as to what happened. Too ashamed to mention I had urinated on the chair, I sat trembling as the assistant turned the saliva ejector back on and dentist resumed drilling. Thankfully, both wore masks that shielded them from the scent of my urine. And, gratefully, my jeans absorbed most even though I felt as if I had jumped into a pond.

Another bladder-bursting disaster occurred while shopping at a supermarket during the premenstrual phase of my cycle. Shortly after grabbing a cart and entering the store, I felt sharp pain in my pelvis. Assuming they were abdominal cramps, I knew I'd have to grin and bear it until I reached home to pop a pill or two.

Clutching my stomach as pain intensified, I made my way to the feminine products aisle to stock up on sanitary pads. As I bent over to grab a second pack, my bladder felt like it had split in two. Although I fought to *hold it* with all my might, urine began streaming down my legs as forceful as a garden hose.

As shoppers strolled past me, I stood soaked and humiliated. Feeling like I was going to croak from embarrassment, I wanted nothing more than to get out of the store as quickly as possible. Therefore, I removed my sweater, wrapped it around my waist, and rushed out of the supermarket infuriated.

Another bladder-brimming episode occurred while standing outside my apartment. Misplacing my keys and unable get in, I dumped contents of my handbag on the door mat to search for them. Without any luck, I went back to my car looking high and low until I realized I had left them on the kitchen counter.

Apparently, none of my neighbors were home since the parking lot of the seven-unit, apartment complex was vacant. Though a golden opportunity to slip between the front end of my car and cement wall to relieve myself, I feared being seen by those living on opposite sides of the building. Therefore, I sat in my car with pulsating bladder spasms as I waited for one my neighbors to arrive.

Seeing a car reel through the security gate approximately twenty minutes later, I wiggled out and asked my neighbor for a screwdriver to unlatch the sliding window lock. As I walked him through the process, having broken into my first-floor apartment once or twice before, my bladder felt full beyond capacity. Then, suddenly, it burst like a water-filled balloon.

Staring as urine penetrated the ground, he nervously said, *"Sorry I'm not moving fast enough."* Several minutes later, he pried the window open, climbed in, and opened the door. Incapable of looking him in the eye as he stepped outside, I thanked him and rushed inside shamed to the core.

In attempt to figure out why I was urinating an average of

twelve times a day, approximately a week before my periods, I first sought to understand how the bladder works. Through research I learned, *"The bladder, located in the pelvis between the pelvic bones, is a hollow, balloon-shaped muscular organ that expands as it fills with urine. The ureters, bladder, and urethra move urine from the kidneys and store it until releasing it from the body. To urinate, the brain signals the muscular bladder wall to tighten, squeezing urine out of the bladder."*[70], according to the National Institute of Diabetes and Digestive and Kidney Diseases.

Even more eye-opening, *"Urinary frequency refers to increased incidence of urge to void. Usually resulting from decreased bladder capacity, frequency is a cardinal sign of a urinary tract infection (UTI). However, it can also stem from another urological disorder, neurologic dysfunction, or pressure on the bladder from a nearby tumor or from organ enlargement (as with pregnancy)."*[71]

---

[70] "The Urinary Tract & How It Works." National Institute of Diabetes and Digestive and Kidney Diseases. Jan. 2014. www.niddk.nih.gov/health-information/urologic-diseases/urinary-tract-how-it-works.

[71] "Rapid Assessment: A Flowchart Guide to Evaluating Signs and Symptoms." p. 390, Lippincott Williams & Wilkins, 2004.

And, after reading a 2001 summary report based on a questionnaire given to 133 women which showed 41% revealed cyclical urinary complaints and 42% had complaints of worsened urinary symptoms prior to their periods.[72], I was led to believe my frequent urination issue was menstrual-related.

Like other PMS and PMDD symptoms I struggled with, I thought it best to first approach treatment from a self-help perspective. Therefore, I reduced my liquid intake to eight glasses per day and ceased consuming liquids four to five hours before sleeping to decrease nighttime urges.

Additionally, I modified my diet by replacing refined sugar and spicy food with cranberries, pumpkin seeds, spinach, and other foods that are said to control frequent urination. And, I drank white vinegar, cranberry juice, and pomegranate juice, all of which claims to treat frequent urination, naturally. However, reduced liquid intake and dietary modifications couldn't rid me of frequent urination misery.

---

[72] Hextall, A., Bidmead, J., et al. "The Impact of the Menstrual Cycle on Urinary Symptoms and the Results of Urodynamic Investigation." *BJOG*, Nov. 2001, Vol. 108, no. 11, pp. 1193-1196, doi.org/10.1111/j.1471-0528.2003.00280.x, Article.

Resorting to over-the-counter medicines with hopes of combating the problem, I experimented with several bladder control medications and patches. While some slightly reduced urinary frequency, most caused unbearable side effects. Instead of drying out my bladder, I ended up dry mouth, dry eyes, and dry skin. Therefore, I halted use of over-the-counter remedies and sought medical attention.

Initially, my doctor ruled out cystitis, irritable bowel syndrome, and prolapsed bladder. Insinuating a bladder infection was likely the cause, he prescribed an antibiotic. However, after completing the seven to ten-day dose with minor side effects, I still urinated every hour on the hour. During a follow up visit, I had hoped he would recommend a pessary, cork, or bladder removal surgery to end the insanity.

With all due respect to doctors whose jobs are to diagnose and prescribe medication based on the process of *elimination*, my health care providers should have recommended a urinary catheter, in my humble opinion. Surely, strapping it to my leg when in public or having it hang off the side of my bed while sleeping, would have utterly destroyed my self-esteem. However, wearing a catheter may have avoided constant trips to the bathroom and dreadful urinary mishaps.

Instead, I was referred to a urologist who found nothing out of the ordinary with my bladder after I underwent a battery of tests. To appease my complaints, he inferred that I had a touch of nervous bladder and prescribed an eight-week supply of bladder control medication. But, after taking them for a few days and experiencing a host of side effects including nausea, headache and dizziness, I stopped.

By age 35, I was so fed up dillydallying with urinary incontinence medication and other remedies, I gave in to wearing demoralizing adult diapers. To avoid saturating clothes, mattresses, couches, chairs, and all else, I would hop into what was originally designed for babies. Although wearing them wounded my confidence, tremendously, I had no other choice than to wear them. Had I not, I would have required a portable toilet or bedpan, especially when overcome with strong urges in wee hours of the night.

My dignity nosedived and self-image plummeted the first time I wore an adult diaper. It was not only demeaning, I felt like I had joined the ranks of the elderly. Although I experimented with various brands of urine collectors to determine which products absorbed my explosions best, I remained in constant fear of leakage and sagging whenever my bladder erupted.

Wearing adult diapers was also a career killer. I remember bending over to pick up a box of manuals to take to the mailroom, while at work. Forgetting to tuck my blouse on the outside of my low-rise pants after using the restroom, I assumed co-workers who also sat in the large cubicle area saw the diaper protruding from my waist. Regardless of whether they caught glimpse of it or not, I was mortified when it happened and for months thereafter.

Another crushing incident occurred while sitting in a saturated diaper at the tail end of a stressful, premenstrual day. Afraid of rising from my soaked, light-blue chair, I waited over fifteen minutes for co-workers who sat in the vicinity of my desk to leave. Squirting hand sanitizer on several sheets yanked out of the tissue box on my desk, I began dabbing as much urine off my chair as I could. I, then, sprinted to the restroom.

The worst urine-escaping, diaper-malfunctioning catastrophe occurred while attending a two-hour, technical writing workshop. Experiencing an overwhelming urge to urinate although I had done so about thirty minutes before it started, I sat contemplating whether I should go to the restroom or wait until the end. Since I didn't want to miss any part of the presentation, I sat squirming in silence, squeezing my pelvic muscles, and performing Kegel exercises.

Approximately an hour before workshop ended, my bladder began raising full-fledged hell. Practically immobilized by intensifying pressure, I stood praying I'd make it to the restroom without incident. However, as soon as I rose to my feet, I flooded my diaper with my skirt bearing the heaviest brunt. Completely doused from waist down, disgraced, and deeply regretting not relieving myself sooner, I trotted to the restroom dying of embarrassment.

Although I wore brands claiming to be highly absorbent, most only held a few ounces which is why urine would escape. Therefore, changing clothes as often as a runway model to avoid smelling like ammonia stench became such a vicious cycle, I began wearing plastic briefs on top of diapers for added protection. Undoubtedly, the amount I spent on diapers and briefs could have afforded me a brand-new bladder.

At a loss as to the exact cause of frequent urination and fearing I'd become a diaper wearer for the rest of my life, I often contemplated startup of an online forum called BabesWithBrimmingBladders.org or something similar. Ranting with multitudes of other socially isolated diaper wearers, like myself, may have reduced the high level of anxiety I felt when hopping in to what felt like a bail of cotton; adjusting to the crackling sounds some brands with plastic backings made; and purchasing adult diapers, in public, which was worse than buying feminine hygiene products.

Seemingly plagued with every premenstrual symptom known to womankind, waging war against frequent urination which caused me to scope out the nearest restroom wherever I went, was *draining*, month after month. Without recommendation to undergo tests to detect any underlying causes of my urinary frequency debacle and since medical treatments either failed to work or had unpleasant side effects, I continued experimenting with remedies such as corn silk, bladderwrack and holy basil supplements. I also performed pelvic muscle exercises, practiced bladder retraining techniques, maintained a routine bathroom schedule, and tracked my fluid intake in attempts to keep my overly excited bladder at bay.

CHAPTER 3
Raging Red Rivers

Clusters of Clogging Clots

Between the age of 28 and 43, the instant I would hear blood sloshing around in my uterus on the second and third days of my periods, I knew bloody hell was about to break loose. Making a beeline to the bathroom, restroom, or portable, with one hand clutching my stomach and the other removing layers of blood absorbers, I'd sit on the toilet with my legs spread apart.

Feeling my vagina stretch as wide as a hippopotamus' mouth, I'd pray the *moment of expulsion* wouldn't be as gut-wrenching as the last. Then, *clunk, plunk, plop, clunk, plunk, plunk, plop, plop* would go the sounds as blood clots, as big as pomegranates, charged out of me. Seconds later, smaller flocks the size of blood oranges, plums and prunes would either sprint or sashay out as if I were passing Santa Claus, his elves, and everyone else who came down the chimney.

Gazing at globs of gruesomeness that either looked like black pudding, eggplant, or Bloodybelly comb jelly performing synchronized swimming stunts, was sheer proof that blood is thicker than water. Causing unfathomable pain before, during, and after ricocheting out of me, it's no wonder I had little interest in having children most of my adult life. If passing blood clots was insufferable, surely, I would not have survived the birthing process.

Passing blood clots was not only painful, the mere sight of them would scare the living daylights out of me. Sometimes, I'd steal a quick glance at the reddish-brownish-purplish, rubbery-looking balls and slabs of vileness. While some appeared to have miniature, translucent veins running through them, others were so ghastly they'd meet their timely doom with an immediate flush.

Although I would strap on multiple sanitary napkins, maternity pads, incontinence diapers, period panties or a combination thereof, some blood clots would ooze out and end up outside the vicinity of most sanitary products. Apparently, some manufacturers fail to include women who bleed like stuck pigs in their product design equation. Therefore, I was forced to stow stockpiles of feminine protection in both handbag and trunk of my car for those just-in-case-I-have-a-bloody-accident moments.

I'll never forget teaching a word processing class at a telecommunications company, in my early 30s. While I dreaded doing so on the second and third day of my periods because of heavy blood flow and contraction-like pain I usually experienced, cancelling the class wasn't an option. In fact, over ten students were registered and most had adjusted their work schedules to attend.

Arriving at around four o'clock that afternoon, I wheeled two large plastic cases filled with student laptops from the parking lot to the classroom. After setting up the equipment, I went back to my car to retrieve a box of training manuals. While reaching across the backseat, I felt as if my uterus was being beaten to a pulp by neighboring reproductive organs.

Writhing in pain, I eased my way onto the driver's seat to calm myself. As I began cursing my periods from as far back as when it first arrived at age 12, with surveillance cameras likely focused on me, blood clots that felt like the size of duck eggs, began plummeting out of me. Placing my left hand under the seat of my pants to ensure both diaper and two maternity pads I wore were in position, I felt wetness on my fingers.

Having a stash of sanitary products and personal hygiene items stored in the trunk, I staggered out, grabbed my mini-suitcase, and returned to the driver's seat. Containing a supply of five diapers, ten maternity or super-size sanitary pads, ten super plus tampons, two pairs of panties, two washcloths, a bar of soap, a roll of toilet paper, a box of sanitary wipes, and plastic bags, surely, I kept my *menstruation suitcase* as replenished as a pantry.

After wiping my hands and dabbing as much blood as I could off both front and back seat of my pants with sanitary wipes, I stepped out of the car. Glancing back and seeing a few stains smeared on the tan-clothed car seat made me shake my head in shame. But, without having the gift of time to clean it, I grabbed the box of manuals and *walked the clot walk* back into the building.

With fifteen minutes left to start the class and to avoid smelling like a beached whale carcass while teaching, I headed to the restroom. After wetting and lathering soap on a washcloth, I eased into a stall and sat on the toilet, praying the bleeding spell would end. As I unpeeled the diaper tabs and saw two saturated pads topped with clumps of clots and resembling road kill, surprisingly, I didn't fall off the seat.

After a cluster of smaller blood clots marched out, I cleaned myself up, changed panties, diapers and maternity pads, tossed all bloody evilness into a plastic bag, and discarded it. Moving as fast as I could to make it to class on time, I blotted as much blood off my pants as possible with wet paper towels and washed my hands.

Naturally, my pants were black as wearing any other color from the waist down was out of the question—including navy blue and dark brown. Even though I looked as if I was attending funerals a few days each month, black pants and skirts were safest, especially since clots commonly escaped past the bundle of sanitary products I wore.

Without being a minute late, I entered the classroom and taught the first half of the four-hour class as blood clots, intermittently, catapulted out of me. During the short break, I wheeled my menstrual suitcase into the restroom and repeated the cleaning and changing process. Mercifully, the last two hours of teaching wasn't as maddening as the first.

The next morning, I called my gynecologist's office and was told to come in when my period was over. Approximately a week later, I discussed my heavy bleeding problem with him. Sounding like a broken record, I shared that birth control pills were ineffective in decreasing my blood flow. Told passing blood clots and heavy bleeding were *normal*, he prescribed a non-steroidal anti-inflammatory medication for pain and insisted I continue taking birth control pills to help reduce blood loss.

Perturbed that he didn't order any tests, I sought the opinions of two other doctors. Being given similar lip service and leaving their offices with neither blood test nor ultrasound recommendations, I had no other choice than to believe my health care providers knew best. Therefore, I did as they instructed by taking prescribed medications and birth control pills, even though I continued having heavy periods.

Determined to find alternative ways to lessen my heavy flow, on my own, I signed up for a membership at a local gym. Since it was effective immediately, I figured I'd stay awhile to familiarize myself with equipment.

Although it wasn't an ideal time to work out being on the second or third day of my period, I was resolute in breaking the cycle of having my heavy bleeding condition hinder me from being active. Likewise, I assumed the chances of having a bloody mishap were slim, considering I had worn two maternity pads that seemingly covered my crotch and derriere twice over, and was planning to stay for only a half hour or so.

With all treadmills in use that busy Saturday afternoon, I

waited roughly twenty minutes before hopping on one. Within seconds of walking, sharp menstrual cramps sat in. As I tried refocusing pain by thinking happy thoughts, my uterus began pulsating and twinges felt like a barrage of blood clots were revving up to storm out of me. Yet, I still refused to let menstrual havoc rain on my parade.

As pain worsened and blood clots begged for baptism, I knew it was time to visit the restroom and pop a pain pill. However, instead of pressing the stop button, I mistakenly pressed the arrow that increases speed. Apparently angry I had done so, blood clots started raging out of me so fast, it felt like the walls of my vagina were being blown out. After pounding on the stop button, the treadmill slowly came to a halt and I went to the restroom.

Inside the stall, I stood facing the toilet so I could guide clots directly into it. Using toilet paper, I gathered a few that had slithered off the pads. And, while plunking them into the toilet, a plum-size clot fell to the floor.

Seeing bare feet on the floor of the adjourning stall and my fallen blood clot a foot or two away caused instant panic. Mortified by what looked like a bloodied, dead rodent lying on the white tiled floor, I stood praying the woman was unaware. But, after several seconds of silence elapsed, I assumed she saw it and was shaken.

At that point, I contemplated whether I should whisper, *"Oops. Sorry about that"* or just let it go. But, out of courtesy, I quickly wound a few sheets of toilet paper around my right hand, snatched it up, and flung it in the toilet as I held onto my crotch with the other to prevent more clots from hitting the floor.

Even though I was bleeding heavily and in sheer pain, I was more concerned about being *found out* by the woman in the neighboring stall. Therefore, I changed pads and raced out of the restroom before she could identify me as the *clot dropper*. Utterly embarrassed by the ordeal, I neither washed my hands nor resumed my workout. In fact, I neither went back to that gym nor any other workout facility ever since.

It was virtually impossible to predict when blood clots were going to catapult out of me, as they weren't on a timer. Regularly stuck on the toilet passing blood clots for long periods, I would try convincing myself I was getting rid of build up from the previous month based on medical books and articles I had read on menstrual blood clots. But, for the life of me, I could never figure out what my body may have been building up since everything, minus my reproductive organs, would come storming out of me most months.

Reading information such as, *"People may worry if they notice clots in their menstrual blood, but this is perfectly normal and rarely cause for concern."*, would make my teeth curl.[73] So much so, I often thought about sitting on the toilet throughout an entire menstrual cycle with a wide-mouth container attached to my vagina. When filled to the hilt, I'd hand it over to both health care providers and researchers to prove statements like, *"In general, women tend to overestimate the amount of blood they lose during a normal period.* (Minkin 30)*"*[74], isn't true for some women with heavy bleeding problems, like myself. In my head, such statements meant my heavy blood loss and pomegranate-size clots were *normal* and I just needed to deal with it.

Information contrary to the volume of blood I was losing also

---

[73] Johnson, J. "Is it Normal to Notice Blood Clots During Your Period?" Medical News Today. 8 Aug. 2018. *MediLexicon, Intl*, www.medicalnewstoday.com/articles/322707.php.

[74] Minkin, MJ. and Wright, CV. "A Woman's Guide to Menopause & Perimenopause." Yale University Press, 2005.

made it impossible to determine if my heavy bleeding was normal or abnormal. And, since health care providers couldn't put a finger on why I was bleeding heavily and passing blood clots, I assumed my chances of bleeding to death was more likely than receiving effective treatment.

Sick and tired of convoluted, limited, or non-responses whenever I'd ask my health care providers, *"How can bleeding this heavy be normal? Could my heavy bleeding mean I have some sort of uterine cancer?* and, *Should I see a specialist or hematologist?"*, I resorted to conducting research to understand why I was bleeding heavily and expelling uterine casts as thick as tri-tip.

When I read an excerpt published in the U.S. National Library of Medicine which stated, *"The typical volume of blood lost during menstruation is approximately 30 mL. Any amount greater than 80 mL is considered abnormal."*[75], I was both enlightened and stumped. Surely, my blood loss appeared far greater than 5.41 tablespoons or 2.70 ounces—the equivalent of 80 milliliters.

---

[75] Reed, BG and Carr, BR. "The Normal Menstrual Cycle and the Control of Ovulation." 5 Aug. 2018. In: De Groot, LJ., Chrousos, G, Dungan K, et al., editors. Endotext [Internet]. South Dartmouth (MA): MDText.com, Inc.; 2000-. www.ncbi.nlm.nih.gov/books/NBK279054, Abstract.

I could also gauge how much blood I was losing by the frequency in changing sanitary pads, maternity pads, diapers, period panties, and all else. And, even after learning "*Menstrual blood is a complex biological fluid composed of blood, vaginal secretions, and the endometrial cells of the uterine wall as they exist immediately prior to menses.*"[76], without a doubt, I was losing at least two cups every thirty minutes or so, especially during heavy flowing days.

As I read scores of medical books, journals, and other literary sources on abnormal bleeding, initially, I thought I had *menorrhagia*, "*...heavy or prolonged menstrual bleeding*" that "*...can be related to a number of conditions including problems with the uterus, hormone problems, or other conditions.*"[77] Since I experienced symptoms of menorrhagia such as bleeding heavily, passing blood clots, and cramping[78], I assumed it was the cause of

---

[76] Yang, H., Zhou, B., et al. "Proteomic Analysis of Menstrual Blood." *Molecular & cellular proteomics*, 2012, Vol. 11, no. 10, pp. 1024-1035, doi.org/10.1074/mcp.M112.018390, Abstract.
[77] "Menorrhagia." Johns Hopkins Medicine. *Health Library*, www.hopkinsmedicine.org/healthlibrary/conditions/gynecological_health/menorrhagia_85,P00571.
[78] "Menorrhagia (Heavy Menstrual Bleeding)." Women's Health Network. 2018. www.womenshealthnetwork.com/pms-and-menstruation/menorrhagia.aspx.

my abnormal bleeding.

Adenomyosis, "...a benign disease of the uterus in which tissues that are usually limited to the endometrium (inner lining of the uterus) are found within the myometrium (the muscular layer of the uterus)"[79], was also a possibility. Assuredly, I experienced many symptoms of the disorder including abnormal bleeding, menstrual cramps, lower abdominal pressure, and bloating. However, several sources claim adenomyosis occurs more often in women over forty who've had children. Since I've never been pregnant, I ruled out the disorder as being the cause of my abnormal bleeding.

Likewise, *endometriosis*, "*...a condition in some women that occurs when the cells that normally line the inside of the uterus (endometrial cells) are found in other parts of the body,"*[80] may have been the culprit as I battled several symptoms of endometriosis

---

[79] "Fibroid-like Conditions: Adenomyosis and Endometrial Polyps." Brigham and Women's Hospital. 2018. www.brighamandwomens.org/obgyn/infertility-reproductive-surgery/cysts-and-fibroids/fibroid-line-conditions-adenomyosis-and-endometrial-polyps.

[80] "Endometriosis Symptoms, Diagnosis and Treatment." Brigham and Women's Hospital. 2018. www.brighamandwomens.org/obgyn/infertility-reproductive-surgery/endometriosis/endometriosis-guide-for-women.

including excessive bleeding, pelvic pain, cramping, and constipation.

I could have also had *uterine fibroid tumors*, *"...also known as uterine myomas, leiomyomas, or fibromas, are firm, compact tumors that are made of smooth muscle cells and fibrous connective tissue that develop in the uterus."*[81] Experiencing many symptoms of fibroids including heavy blood flow, painful periods, abdominal and lower back pain, bloating, constipation, and frequent urination made the disorder a likelihood, as well.

But since health care providers placed *band aids* on my complaints of heavy bleeding, instead of ordering tests to pinpoint the cause, I continued bleeding profusely during my periods.

---

[81] "Fibroids." UCLA Obstetrics and Gynecology. 2018. UCLA Health, www.obgyn.ucla.edu/fibroids.

Epitome of Embarrassing Episodes

While stocking up on period paraphernalia, I would sometimes glare at miniature boxes of panty liners. I'd stand in the aisle wishing I was one of those lucky women whose periods are as light as a scraped knee. But, once reality sat it, I'd zoom in on the *super-duper* blood absorbers I, unluckily, had to wear to handle the volume of blood and clots that spewed out of me.

Economically taxing and equivalent to a month's worth of groceries, I usually purchased two of the largest bags of sanitary pads; a pack of maternity pads; a pack of adult diapers; and two boxes of tampons, each month. Although store brands were cheaper, experience taught me to never wear generic feminine products, especially sanitary and maternity pads. They not only lacked adequate absorbency, they would twist, bunch, and end up in areas other than the center of my underwear and diapers.

Even with quality products stacked between my legs someone, usually a stranger, was bound to pull me aside and whisper, *"There's something on your skirt, Miss."* With heavy menstrual bleeding causing leaks at the wrong times and in the wrong places, I would often dodge family get-togethers and cancel social events. In the back of my mind I'd think, *"They should thank their lucky stars I was a no-show. No doubt, I would've turned their ivory dining chairs ruby-red; lodged blood clots between their cream-colored couch cushions; and left a trail of crimson droplets on their beige Berber carpet on the way out!"*

At a relatively young age, I learned what it's like to be humiliated in public while menstruating. Wearing a white top, white baggy jeans, and white sneakers to junior high school one day, I thought I was the cutest girl in the world. I felt even more beautiful after receiving compliments from my school friends, most of whom lived on my block in Brooklyn, New York.

While walking home from school, we heard a couple of boys giggling as they trailed behind us. Unsure as to why they were laughing and hoping they'd stop, we turned around and stared them down for a few seconds.

In recognizing one of the boys, although I didn't know his name, I became even more upset. A week prior, he had made fun of my skin color by calling me *"blackie"*, several times, as I walked home alone. At first, I thought he was just flirting with me. But, realizing he was being mean-spirited, I was angry yet curious as to why he kept calling me such a name. I loved my dark skin and was proud of it. Surely, he must've known that I loved my dark skin and was proud of it. I was also popular from performing in plays and being in special classes for bright students, I thought.

Thankfully, the laughter stopped once they turned the corner. And, as soon as I arrived home, I went to the bathroom. In pulling my pants down and seeing huge, dark red bloodstains in the seat and back of them, I wanted to shrivel up and die. Knowing my bloody stains were the reason why the boys were laughing hysterically, embarrassed me to tears. The thought of being at school all day with three, quarter-sized spots, made me feel even worse.

Crying to no end while bathing, I kept envisioning the entire school gossiping about me and feared being laughed if I returned the next morning. Had I followed my mother's advice on double-checking my pads every hour when I first began menstruating at age 12, I would've saved myself from humiliation, I thought.

Though the incident lingered in my head for hours, I was too ashamed to tell my mother or anyone else what had happened. However, later that evening, I told my older brother who was always protective of me and practiced several forms of martial arts. Tearfully mentioning the laughter and name calling, without going into detail about the bloodstains, he quickly turned away and said something like, *'I'll meet you after school tomorrow, so you can point the boy out to me."*

At dismissal time, the next day, I walked out of the building and searched for my brother. As he stood in a sea of students, I pointed out the boy who laughed because of my menstrual incident and called me a disparaging name. And, what happened next was much like the scene in *The Godfather*[82], where Carlo gets beaten to a pulp by his wife's brother, Sonny, as payback for mercilessly abusing his wife Connie.

As he beat the living daylights out of the boy, my brother beckoned me over. Slowly inching toward them, he made the boy apologize to me as he continued roughing him up. Lying on the ground with a bloody nose and hundreds of students looking on, certainly, he felt as ashamed and humiliated as I had. Thereafter, I

---

[82] *The Godfather*, written by Mario Puzo, directed by Francis F. Coppola, performances by Brando, Marlon, Al Pacino, James Caan, Robert Duvall, Talia Shire, and Diane Keaton, Paramount Home Video, 1972.

became even more popular as, seemingly, everyone wanted to be friends with me, especially boys.

In retrospect, the embarrassment of being in public with bloodstained pants as a middle schooler was minor compared to humiliating incidents that occurred as an adult. One such episode happened while driving home with my roommate from a nightclub on the *first night* of my period. Assuming dancing all night may have triggered heavy bleeding, several hours earlier than usual, we stopped at a gas station so I could use the restroom. Having a single sanitary napkin in my purse because I had anticipated a light flow that evening, I wound a bunch of toilet paper and placed it inside my panties for added protection—praying it wasn't laced with germs.

Throughout the hour-long ride home, my uterus and abdomen throbbed as we talked about the great time we had and guys we met. Turning into the driveway to park, I reached for my purse I had placed on the floor mat. Upon sitting erect, blood and clots began barging out of me. Petrified and embarrassed, I told my roommate that I was bleeding heavily and may have saturated her car seat.

Slowly stepping out, I held both hands under my crotch to prevent blood from causing more damage. While walking up the first flight of stairs, our next-door neighbors and crowd of friends waved from their balcony and invited us to join them. With my hands buried between my thighs, I could neither respond nor wave back as I moved as fast as I could up the second flight of stairs.

Terribly embarrassed and temporarily handicapped, my roommate assisted me to my bathroom. Had she not, both bedroom and bathroom doors would have looked like part of a slasher film set. And, once showered and protected with a gang of blood absorbers, I gathered cleaning supplies, a flashlight, and her car key, and scrubbed every inch of the bloody mess I had made at, approximately, three o'clock in the morning.

Another menstruation-gone-bad incident occurred while at the beach with my boyfriend. Thanks to birth control pills, my period arrived a few days earlier than expected. To avoid looking as if I had grown a pubic afro by wearing a bulky, sanitary pad inside my multi-colored bikini bottom, I protected myself with a tampon instead. I also brought along extra tampons to prevent a leakage incident and a dark-colored beach towel.

Although I rarely went to the beach during menstruation, my boyfriend thought it was a good way to relieve menstrual tension. After building a rather odd-looking sand castle for thirty minutes or so, he went for a swim and I sprawled out on my beach towel to relax.

Moments later, I began flooding. With my tampon sliding out of my vagina, I walked as fast as I could to the restroom. As blood began flowing heavier, I glanced between my legs and saw that it had soaked through the seat of my bikini bottom. Therefore, I wrapped the beach towel around my waist and continued walking toward the restroom.

Once inside, I flung open vacant stall doors, like a madwoman, in search of toilet paper. Finding none and beating myself up for not bringing a roll along with me, as usual, I had no other choice than to use my beach towel. And, as my luck would have it, there wasn't any soap in the dispensers, so I ran cold water over the towel and rushed inside the stall.

After cleaning myself up and changing tampons, my next challenge was figuring out how I was going to clean my bikini bottom without other women noticing my menstrual misfortune.

Launching into survival mode, I removed my bikini bottom and covered my lower half with the bloodied towel. Moving to the sink, I washed it in cold water. Once somewhat clean, I went back into the stall to put it on then returned to the sink to clean bloody sections of the towel.

Both overwhelmed and frustrated, I walked out of the restroom and into the waiting arms of my boyfriend. When he said, "*I knew I'd find you here. Are you okay?*", I burst into tears because he knew how difficult it was for me in coping with my heavy bleeding condition and preventing demoralizing, menstrual incidents.

Seemingly plagued with blood-leaking catastrophes, menstruation took a tremendous toll on my social life and made me anxiety-riddled, overtime. By my mid-30's, I feared social events, especially after the unforgettable *beach incident*. Regardless of my usually consistent pattern of *non-heavy days*, I thought it in my best interest to remain homebound throughout the entire length of my periods.

Rarely did I chance socializing even on *safer days*. However, on one such occasion I attended a pool party on the fourth day of my period. Since my heavy blood flow usually began tapering off by this time, I figured laying out in my bathing suit and being around people would help overcome my fear of being in public during menstruation.

When I arrived, there were around fifty people who were either mingling around the huge deck or swimming in the Olympic-size pool. As I munched on appetizers and sipped a glass of wine, I shared with a male friend who had invited me that I never learned how to swim.

Convincing me that it would only take a few minutes to teach me the basics, I was elated and protected, so in the pool I went. First showing me how to kick my feet while keeping them straight, seemed easier than I ever imagined. He, then, demonstrated how I should move my arms one at a time. Pulling me closer to the deep end and requesting I try swimming on my own, I resisted with fear of drowning. However, he assured me he'd hold onto my body as I swam.

After guiding me from one side of the pool to the other a few times, he let go and I began swimming on my own. Shouting, *"Yay! I'm swimming!"*, he and others in the pool and on the deck began clapping. Thrilled to finally learn how to swim, especially with an audience cheering me on, I smiled from ear-to-ear and didn't want to get out.

However, as I embarked on another lap, my friend swam toward me and whispered, *"Rose, I think something…"* Unable to make out what he was saying likely because I was splashing water a bit much, he pulled me closer toward him and said, *"You must be having your period because I see a little blood in the pool."* As he pointed to the albeit, faint trail of redness a few inches away, I was mortified to the point of wanting to swim to the deep end and drown.

Overwhelmingly humiliated in having blood seep past a super-size tampon and in front of all those people, I hurriedly stepped out of the pool. After putting on my sundress and easing my way to the bathroom, I left without saying goodbye to anyone—not even my friend who graciously invited me to his pool party and taught me how to swim.

Menstrual mishaps seemed to progressively worsen as I became older. At age 36, I remember grabbing a bite at the food court, during my lunch break, and sitting on a white, plastic chair within the patio area. While eating, I could feel blood and clots going berserk inside my uterus. Since I had just changed my sanitary pads and diaper a few minutes' prior, I just dealt with the discomfort.

With pain causing me to lose my appetite, I stood and tossed my half-eaten salad in the garbage. And, as soon as I did, my vagina felt like hefty meat balls were charging out of it. Seeing smudges of blood on the chair, I thought, *"Not again. Lord, please. Not again."*

Darting inside the office building and seeing a swarm of people in the lobby, I panicked. *'There's no way I'm getting on that elevator with a nest of blood clots between my legs.'*, I thought. Therefore, I eased past the crowd and walked up seven flights of stairs to use the company's restroom that required badge entry. Once inside, I was so exhausted and bloody, it took the remaining of my lunch break to clean myself up.

Yet, another daunting incident occurred at a movie theatre. On day five of my period which meant it was practically over, my boyfriend and I had gone to see a film. As we stood in line to buy refreshments, I felt a strong surge of blood leave my body. Anguished because I didn't anticipate such heavy outpour at this stage of my period, I told my boyfriend I needed to use the restroom and would meet him inside the theatre.

Looking in the mirror, I saw a bloodstain the size of a golf ball and smudges on the back of my light-colored jeans. How blood travels from the crotch to the buttocks area always boggled my mind. I also freaked out because I didn't know if others saw the stain while walking from the parking lot to the concession stand.

As I moved inside the stall, I neither knew what to do nor how I was going to remove the stain. Heavy flowing traffic in and out of the restroom made me even more anxious. However, in forcing myself to relax so I could come up with a plan, I realized that I had to let go of my pride, resist fear of embarrassment, and get to the sink.

Being as inconspicuous as possible, I walked out of the stall with my hands covering my backside; yanked several paper towels from the dispenser and ran cold water over them; then headed inside a vacant one. After replacing my pad, I balled up handfuls of toilet tissue and placed it inside my panties for added protection.

In removing most blood with the wet paper towels, I left noticeable, damp spots on my jeans. Having to swallow my pride,

I washed my hands and headed inside the theater. Sitting with a perplexed look on his face, my boyfriend asked what took so long. Too embarrassed to tell him about my bloody fiasco, I mentioned that I had a bad bout of diarrhea as the opening credits rolled.

The most unforgettable and downright humiliating bleeding episode occurred on an airplane. Working as a consultant for a retail company, I was required to fly to Colorado to assist in the development of a company-wide, training project. Though deathly afraid of flying on the third day of my period, the quick turnaround itinerary made me somewhat at ease. I was scheduled to arrive the same morning of travel, stay until late afternoon, and head back to California that evening, thankfully.

Shortly after boarding the plane, I prayed that I'd survive the roughly two-hour flight without a menstrual catastrophe, then nodded off since I had little rest the night before. However, within thirty minutes or so, I was awakened by pulsating pain and clumps of clots spouting out of me.

Discreetly performing a touch test to see if blood had seeped onto the seat of my pants, I saw smudges on my fingertips and panicked. Being trapped in the window seat with two male passengers asleep on my left was equally unnerving. But, knowing I had to get to the restroom immediately, I tapped the shoulder of the passenger beside me, who awoke and moved to the aisle, as did the other passenger.

Upon standing, more blood clots shot out of me faster than speeding bullets. As I struggled to pull my carry-on suitcase out of the overhead compartment, a flight attendant sprinted down the aisle and demanded that I return to my seat. Glaring at her with utter contempt, I whispered *"I'm bleeding heavily and need to use the restroom."* Without regard to my plea, she pointed to a nearby *fasten seat belt sign* and insisted that I return to my seat, until it was turned off.

Shocked by her response to my bloody, mid-air crisis, I felt like removing my diaper and two maternity pads and shoving it in her face to prove I was having an emergency. Instead, I gave her a lethal stare that made her, finally, back off.

Hauling the suitcase, at crotch level, so passengers seated in the aisles wouldn't catch whiff, I walked toward the back of the small aircraft, a sweaty, smelly, bloody mess. Surprisingly, blood and clots didn't trickle down my pant legs and land on the cabin floor while en route to the restroom.

Once inside, things turned from bad to worse. With strong turbulence causing me to rock back and forth, removing my bloodied pants, pamper and pads seemed to take forever. After placing heaps of covers on the toilet seat, I sat hoping each forceful flush would suck the blood clots out of me.

Unable to find the bar of soap I packed, I had to pump globs of foaming hand soap onto my washcloth. And, since my plastic bag of bloody items including my pants couldn't fit inside the small opening of the waste bin, I had to put it in my suitcase.

Thereafter, I must've strapped on so many feminine protection products, one would've thought I was preparing for a long mission into outer space. And, as I changed into the extra pair of pants, all I could think about was having a wad of cash, so I could bribe the pilot into turning the plane around and dropping my bloody butt off at my doorstep.

Basking in Bloody Baths

Often brought to my knees by heavy menstrual flow and cramps, I'd plug myself up with the largest tampons on the market, light a candle, and submerge in blistering bubble baths. While waiting for temporary relief, erratic pushing and gushing sensations would usually set in. Minutes later, blood matter would come storming out of me with such force, I'd end up lying in a cesspool of blood, clots, red bubbles, and inflated tampons as big as sheep.

Nauseated by rubbery chunks, resembling dwarfed orange roughies, encircling me, I'd attempt to catch them with a washcloth or sponge as they pounced about. Those that slithered out of reach were met with *the cup* I, customarily, used to nab and flush the unsightly things down the toilet. After changing *plugs* and showering, I'd clean, drain, and redraw another bath to take the edge off my horrendous periods.

My heavy bleeding conundrum caused so many bathing-related incidents, it's impossible to say which was most unsettling. I remember sitting on the toilet for what seemed like an hour, grasping my stomach, rocking back and forth, and hearing blood rain and clots splash. Feeling hopeless, helpless and desperate for relief, I drew a tub of hot water as soon as my heavy flow dissipated.

Upon stepping in, I realized that I had forgotten to insert a tampon. Therefore, I stepped out and reached inside the cabinet beneath the sink to get one. In doing so, humongous blood clots, ranging in size of prunes to passion fruit, began raging out of me. Trying my best to endure the all too common scenario which was physically and mentally draining, I hopped back onto the toilet and waited for the remaining clan of clots to expel. And, once expulsion tapered, I cleaned myself up, inserted a new tampon, and laid in the tub until pain dwindled.

Another blood bath episode occurred while lying in bed, one evening, with pounding pelvic pain and droves of blood clots shooting out of me. Unable to tolerate pain which felt like a host of King crab trapped inside my uterus and hell-bent on clawing their way, I ate a slice of bread to prevent nausea, then took pain medication. As I sat in the tub waiting for the pills to kick in, I passed out. Awoken, hours later, to blood clots gallivanting in a hue of red water as if I had been bludgeoned, I quickly drained the tub and showered.

While the aftermath of taking hot baths was maddening, it seemed like the best way to cope with uncontrollable bleeding and cramping during menstruation. Assuredly, I tried everything from lying down to sitting upright, in the tub, to prevent blood and clots from either escaping past tampons or ejecting, entirely. I even started wearing both tampon and plastic adult diaper to avoid blood baths. Although they were cumbersome and would end up sopping wet, I didn't have any choice.

I'll never forget waking wee hours in the night to excruciating menstrual cramps and belligerent blood clots that were gearing up for release. Shooting out of bed to seek refuge in the tub, I ran hot water on full blast. And, after inserting a tampon and strapping on a diaper, believing the later would stop the tampon from being cast out with blood clots, I popped two pain pills and immersed my body in the bathtub.

As cramping intensified and clots began knocking about my uterus, I sensed a blood surge was well underway. Although I tried tightening my vaginal muscles to hold back the impending flow, clots came barging out of me so forcefully, I had to hold onto my diapered crotch to prevent a disaster. Using the grab bar, I lifted myself to my feet and stepped out. Upon peeling back the diaper tabs, I saw what looked like a gaggle of pickled beets and a vaguely recognizable tampon. Shaking my head in utter fear and disgust, I cleaned myself up, changed my tampon and diaper, and drew another bath.

As a heavy bleeder, it was a challenge finding *water-proof* products that provided protection while bathing during menstruation. Although aware of menstrual cups that claim to be ideal for heavy flowing periods, I had reservations about using them. I didn't believe they could hold the amount of blood that poured out of me. And, I was equally concerned about the high-maintenance aspects of the product such as cleaning it with soap and water after each use and boiling it once a month for sanitary purposes. I was also repulsed by the idea of having silicone inside my vagina. But, since I had to bathe and shower more than usual during my periods, I purchased a four-pack containing two small and two large menstrual cups, out of desperation.

Knowing the larger one would be impossible, I made several attempts in inserting the small cup. However, neither the folding method nor any other technique would lodge the menstrual cup in place. Deeply discouraged and fed up with getting blood everywhere, I waited until my next cycle to give it another try.

Even after successfully inserting it, I was met with the challenge of moving it around the rim to ensure it opened properly. And, removing it was even more untoward. While the instructions recommended squatting and bearing down to pull the nozzle downward so contents could pour into the toilet, I had to wear gloves and use a wad to toilet paper to avoid staining the linoleum.

Furthermore, dumping large clots into the toilet was more distressing and laborious than I ever imagined. Therefore, I tossed the four-pack of menstrual cups, as I likely needed a pail to collect the amount of blood and clots that dropped out of me, during most periods. Without any luck in finding sanitary products, specifically, designed for bathing and showering during menstruation, made me often wonder if bathing *during that time of the month* was hygienically correct.

While researching the subject, I stumbled upon several myths and taboos such as bathing during menstruation can negatively affect women's health; showering with hot water, while menstruating, will cause heavy flow; lying down can prevent menstrual blood from flowing out; and wearing a tampon, while bathing, can cause toxic shock syndrome through bacterial infection.

Regardless, seeking refuge in the bathtub was the best means of easing my menstrual horrors. Albeit extreme, immersing my body in hot baths, two or more times a day, was how I coped. I'd even pour a few pots of boiling water into drawn baths, as the hotter the water, the sooner excruciating pain seemed to dwindle.

Once, in menstrual purgatory in the middle of the night, I remember emptying two large pots of boiling water into a partially drawn bath. After downing two pain relievers, *tamponing* and *diapering*, I stepped in and sat praying for relief.

Continually redrawing hot water for an hour or so, yet to no avail, I stepped out and laid on the living room floor in ripping pain. Fearing neighbors in the quaint, seven-unit apartment complex would call the police for disturbing the peace or an ambulance to cart me to the emergency room, I buried my face in throw pillows and roared to no end.

Pain was so agonizing, neither I nor my dog could sleep. Having instincts of a human and hearing my cries of anguish, he began licking my tears away. Giving me strength to rise to my feet, moments later, I returned to the kitchen and boiled two more pots of water, hoping to stamp out pain. Eventually falling asleep in the sizzling tub, I awoke hours later without pain and the tub didn't look like a bloody crime scene. Lying in bed with my dog close by my side, I slept until noon.

The following evening, a neighbor who had recently moved in, expressed concern about constant running water that early morning and asked if I was okay. Too embarrassed to mention that I, regularly, took lengthy baths to cope with my abnormal menstrual bleeding and cramping disorders, I said something similar to, *'Sorry, but my dog, Prince, ended up with a terrible bout of diarrhea after getting hold of a piece of chocolate while walking him late, last night. Therefore, I had to give him a nice, long bath.'*, instead.

Taking scorching baths to alleviate menstrual hell once proved dangerous when I awoke to ridiculously heavy bleeding and debilitating cramps, one morning. With only an hour to calm pain and get dressed before heading to work, I boiled two large pots of water. After emptying the first into the tub of hot running water, I returned to the stove to retrieve the second pot. However, while en route to the bathroom, I tripped on the bath rug.

Gratefully, holding the pot with my arms extended forward prevented me from scalding myself, although a few splashes landed on my right hand. After running cold water on it to ease stinging and blistering, I tossed the rest of the water in the tub and laid in it as pain subsided quicker than usual.

From that point forward, I forewent adding boiling water to baths; immersing in them for hours at a time; as well as taking two or more of baths each day of my periods. Evidently, looking like a shriveled prune with skin as dry as seaweed and ending up with relentless itching, as if I had contracted a bad case of Norwegian scabies, was as clearly unhealthy.

At age 38, I remember walking to a coffee shop that was approximately two miles away from home. In less than ten minutes, I felt like a swarm of blood-thirsty mosquitoes were sucking the life out of the lower half of my body. Needle-like poking and burning sensations first began in my thighs, then quickly radiated to my buttocks. Stopping me dead in my tracks, I stood on the sidewalk of a busy boulevard scratching myself silly.

As the itching gradually subsided, I contemplated whether I

should continue walking to the coffee shop or head home. But, knowing another flare-up was bound to occur regardless of which direction I went in, I headed toward the coffee shop. Slowing my pace to preempt another attack, I walked approximately a half mile before irritating, itching sensations started up again.

` The need to scratch was so intense that by the time I arrived, I sat on the patio for nearly twenty minutes, clawing at my skin before going inside to buy a cup of coffee. Dreading the walk home, I decided to jog instead so I could make it home sooner. However, itching agony shortly followed suit and I ran as fast as I could. Once home, I tore my clothes off and laid in a tub of warm water for a couple of minutes.

Noticing patterns of irritating itching every time I took shorts walks, especially on *light days* of my periods, I assumed my bathing ritual was the cause. Therefore, I saw a doctor who suggested my reactions were likely due to a lack of regular exercise. Surely, she was on point, as I found it nearly impossible to do much of anything while struggling with abnormally heavy bleeding, cramps and other menstrual issues.

In further explaining that I was likely experiencing exercise-induced histamine reactions and later learning, *"Exercise-induced urticaria and cold-induced urticaria may cause elevated plasma histamine levels coincident with the onset of pruritus and hives."*[83], I began exercising as much as I could and taking anti-histamines thirty minutes prior—to lessen the severity of itching as if being attacked by cacti. I also scaled back, significantly, on taking baths during menstruation.

Losing such an excessive amount of blood, most months, may have also caused iron-deficiency anemia, *"…usually due to blood loss but may occasionally be due to poor absorption of iron."*[84], according to American Society of Hematology. For years, I experienced many common symptoms of anemia including shortness of breath, light-headedness, insomnia, brittle nails, and cracked lips. I also experienced stunted hair growth which forced me to fill in the blanks with either wiglets or hair weaves.

Unfortunately, symptoms of anemia lingered well into my

---

[83] Silvers, WS. "Exercise-induced Allergies: The Role of Histamine Release." *Ann Allergy*, Jan. 1992, Vol. 68, no. 1, pp. 58-63, *PubMed.gov*, www.ncbi.nlm.nih.gov/pubmed/?term=Silvers%20WS%5BAuthor%5D&cauthor=true&cauthor_uid=1371041, Abstract.
[84] "Anemia." American Society of Hematology. 2018. www.hematology.org/Patients/Anemia/.

40s since a *complete blood count (CBC*), a test that counts the number blood cells in sample blood, specifically red blood cell levels in blood (hematocrit) and hemoglobin when testing for anemia.[85], wasn't ordered until then. In fact, results of the final report revealed my iron stores were disastrously low. While normal range for women is between 45-180, my iron count was 8 grams per deciliter. My hematocrit was a low 19.9, with normal range being 35-47. And, my hemoglobin count was a critically low 5.7, whereby the normal range for women is, generally, 11-16.

Being officially diagnosed with chronic anemia, I was prescribed ferrous sulfate, an iron supplement that boosts iron levels and folic acid.[86] Additionally, I made drastic dietary changes by increasing my intake of iron-rich foods. I ate beef liver, oysters and sardines, all of which are said to good sources of *heme iron,* a type of iron which maintains healthy levels and is better absorbed

---

[85] "Anemia." Mayo Clinic. 8 Aug. 2017. www.mayoclinic.org/diseases-conditions/anemia/diagnosis-treatment/drc-20351366.

[86] Johnson-Wimbley, TD. and Graham, DY. "Diagnosis and Management of Iron Deficiency Anemia in the 21st Century." *Therap Adv Gastroenterol*, 2011, Vol. 4, no. 3, pp. 177-84, doi:10.1177/1756283X11398736, Abstract.

than non-heme iron that's found in plants and iron-fortified foods.[87] I also ate white beans, Kidney beans, chickpeas, and spinach.

But, despite eating iron-rich foods and consuming iron supplements, daily, to boost levels to normal range, my iron stores remained low. Apparently, my body wasn't producing hemoglobin fast enough to compensate for, seemingly, pints of blood lost during my periods. Therefore, correcting anemia was virtually impossible.

Perhaps, blood transfusion may have helped in restoring my blood count levels based on an article published in the Journal of Blood Transfusion which states, *"Subjects with Hb concentrations below 6 g/dL almost always require transfusion therapy."*[88] Considering my hemoglobin count was 5.7 and my bloody floods would often leave me so weak, dizzy and discombobulated that the thought of robbing a blood bank seemed logical, clearly, I was a candidate. However, my health care providers neither

---

[87] Johnson-Wimbley, TD. and Graham, DY. "Diagnosis and Management of Iron Deficiency Anemia in the 21st Century." *Therap Adv Gastroenterol*, 2011, Vol. 4, no. 3, pp. 177-84, doi:10.1177/1756283X11398736, Abstract.

[88] Liumbruno, G., Bennardello F., et al. "Recommendations for the Transfusion of Red Blood Cells." *Blood Transfus*, 2009, Vol. 7, no. 1, pp. 49-64, doi:10.2450/2008.0020-08.

recommended nor ordered blood transfusion.

It's no wonder I, practically, lived in bathrooms and restrooms during menstruation. Having no control over volumes of blood and clots that stormed out of me, most months, even after consuming what seemed like lifetime supplies of iron supplements, birth control pills, and prescription pain medication, was rather piteous, throughout my late 20s to early 40s.

CHAPTER 4

Dwellers in the Downstairs Department

Pap and Pelvic Exam Pandemonium

Not only was I tortured by heavy bleeding, I developed *membranous dysmenorrhea*, a disorder involving *"...the spontaneous slough of the endometrium in one cylindrical or membranous piece that retains the shape of the uterine cavity."*[89] Although claimed a *rare* disorder, single membranous pieces referred to as an *endometrial*, *uterine* or *decidual casts*[90], plummeted out of me twice.

At age 35, I expelled one while attempting to paint the town *red* on a Saturday evening. My girlfriend, her parents, and I had gone to a nightclub in Los Angeles, California. Although it was the third day of my period, I figured a bloody catastrophe was unlikely since I had visited the restroom upon arrival. Noticing I wasn't flowing heavily after changing my tampon and maternity pads, I felt confident and protected.

Though I dreaded being in public during my unrelenting

---

[89] Rabinerson, D., Kaplan, B., et al. "Membranous Dysmenorrhea: The Forgotten Entity." *Obstet Gynecol,* May 1995, Vol. 85, no. 5 Pt 2, pp. 891-892, doi:10.1016/0029-7844(94)00302-T, Abstract.

[90] Malik, MF., Adekola, H., et al. "Passage of Decidual Cast Following Poor Compliance with Oral Contraceptive Pill." *Fetal and Pediatric Pathology,* 2015, Vol. 34, no. 2, pp. 103-107, doi.org/10.3109/15513815.2014.970263, Abstract.

periods, I was thrilled to be out of the house and enjoying life for a change. And, I must've danced for nearly a half hour before sitting to chitchat with my friend and her parents. However, as soon as I did, I felt cramping pain and blood clots jockeying for position. Several minutes later, I felt tugging sensations as if my uterus was being tied with a rope.

As I tried breathing through pain and discomfort, a tall, handsome man to whom I was ready to say *"I do"*, asked me to dance. In attempting to stand, sharp pain began cascading through my pelvis and lower back. Surely, he must have thought I was paralyzed while helping me to my feet. But, unable to handle the insane pain, I mentioned something on par with, *"I'm sorry, but I think I have a charley horse in my calf"* and sat back down as he walked away perplexed.

When blood clots began somersaulting inside my uterus, I hauled tail to the restroom. Standing in line for roughly ten minutes, I discreetly grasped my pelvis that felt as hard as a rock. Once I made it inside the stall, pain became so excruciating, it took forever to pull my panties below my hips.

Within seconds of sitting on the toilet, a large slab of

something spiraled out of me. As I shot off the toilet, I saw what looked like a head of a newborn calf. Standing in sheer anguish, I tried to decipher whether I should leave the massive thing lodged in the toilet or flush it with a chance of causing a flood. Surely, the restroom attendant who appeared well in her 60s, would have gone into cardiac arrest had she discovered the gruesome-looking thing while cleaning, I thought. Therefore, I flushed it down the pipes, hoping it wouldn't cause a backup and would end up in the bowels of hell for destroying my evening.

At age 39, I passed a second uterine cast after sitting doubled-over on the toilet unleashing blood clots to no end. As my uterus began stretching beyond comprehension, it felt like a grenade had detonated inside me. Then, suddenly, a V-shaped, fleshy mass that resembled a slice of bloodied pizza topped with liver, plunged out of me. Traumatized and convinced my uterus was possessed, I looked in the toilet and saw the humongous object parlaying amongst blood and clots.

With a brush of bravery, after spending nearly ten minutes trying to figure out what it was, I put on a plastic glove and removed it. Not only was I high on curiosity, I wanted to hand the ginormous mass over to my doctor so he wouldn't think I was hallucinating. But, unable to stomach the sight of it, I threw it in a plastic bag, cleaned myself up, and took it straight to the dumpster.

Once my period was over, I went to my primary care physician's office, without a scheduled appointment. After explaining what had happened, he initially insisted I passed several large blood clots that were nestled together. Informing him that the massive piece of flesh looked nothing like blood clots, he suspected miscarriage.

Confounded and feeling as if he had mistaken me for one of his pregnant patients, I tried to convince him I wasn't pregnant; have never been pregnant; and couldn't possibly be pregnant since sex was the last thing on my mind with all the *female issues* I had. Finally, he mentioned I may have passed a uterine cast and scheduled an appointment for an annual physical exam.

I loathed the Pap smear portion of these exams. Although important in detecting *human papillomavirus (HPV),* a common sexually transmitted virus which can cause cervical and other types of cancers[91], I could never wrap my brain around why my vaginal walls had to be stretched as wide as a yawning baboon—just to collect a smidgen of cervical tissue. And, once the harrowing ordeals were over, I'd walk like a bow-legged cowgirl from the exam table to the parking lot.

Preparing for annual physicals was much like getting ready for a date. While showering, I'd shave my armpits and legs to circumvent being mistaken for a Siberian cat. After salving my body with petroleum jelly to mask my ashy skin, I'd sit on the toilet with a hand mirror and shave myself bald to avoid looking like a curly-haired pigeon *down there*. Then, I'd soak my feet in a basin and give myself a pedicure, just to give my doctor assurance that I was human and not a grizzly bear.

Having a relatively small practice with roughly five exam rooms, I was told to wait in one that was cold enough to cause hypothermia, until his assistant escorted me into the hallway to be weighed. Upon returning, she placed a thermometer under my

---

[91] "Genital HPV Infection - Fact Sheet: What is HPV?" 16 Nov. 2017. Centers for Disease Control and Prevention, www.cdc.gov/std/hpv/stdfact-hpv.htm.

tongue and began asking off-the-wall questions like, *'Are you sexually active?'* Giving her a look potent enough to kill bed bugs, since I had shared with both her and the doctor that my gynecological issues made sex so atrocious I had taken a hiatus, during past visits, I responded by shaking my head.

Quickly removing the thermometer, she jotted down information on my chart and handed me an exam gown, evidently, made of one hundred percent tissue. Looking like a scantily clad, paper doll, I sat on the exam table with my derriere partially exposed. Normally, I'd look for creases in the paper before sitting, as the last thing I needed was to contract germs and diseases of those who likely sat bare-bottomed on the same paper. But, since I was freezing to death, I let it go.

When the knock finally came, I greeted my doctor as he entered with his assistant. In asking the purpose of my visit, I reminded him that a huge, dense piece of flesh had barged out of me for the second time and that I was due for an annual exam.

Instructing me to lay on my back, he began touching my breasts as if endangered species, to check for lumps, bumps or growths. After spending a few seconds on each, he requested that

I scoot my frozen bottom as close to the edge of the exam table as possible; separate my knees; and place my feet in the metal stirrups. With all sense of dignity flying out the window, I complied as he rolled his stool closer, positioned the movable lamp, then dropped out of sight.

As he peered into my vaginal doors, he whispered in a low voice, *"Come closer. A little more. More. Great. Now, take a deep breath and relax. It'll just take a minute."* Frightening the living daylights out of me, I wiggled my toes to ease nervous tension as he usually instructed me to do.

Being a regular patient, he should have known the combination of his murmuring and repetitive butt-scooting requests traumatized me. I'd become so scared, the thought of stepping out of the stirrups, butt-walking my way off the exam table, and running for my life, would always cross my mind. However, I tried calming myself by closing my eyes and thinking happy thoughts while clutching onto his assistant's hand.

Taking deep breaths to maintain my composure, he first performed the *external exam* in which he inspected my lower abdomen for signs of tenderness, masses, and other abnormalities.[92] However, as soon as he eased the super-size speculum that looked more like a duck's bill, as far as it could go, and stretched me wide enough for him to crawl in, I began squealing like a hyena.

Then, he inserted a long spatula resembling a tongue depressor and instrument called a *cytobrush* that looked no different than an eyelash primer brush, to collect sample tissue from my cervix. Hearing the eerie clamping sound of the speculum and being swabbed with what felt like a miniature rake, not only sent me through the roof, my body began tensing up, again. And, after a few minutes of teeth-clenching discomfort, he removed the Pap smear gadgets.

Before I could exhale, he placed two gloved fingers inside me, though it felt like his entire hand, and began pressing on my abdomen. Called a *bimanual exam* which checks the size and shape of the uterus, ovaries, and other organs as well as detects

---

[92] Long, WN. "Pelvic Examination." In: Walker, HK., Hall, WD., Hurst, JW., editors. Clinical Methods: The History, Physical, and Laboratory Examinations. 3rd edition. Chap. 177, Boston: Butterworths, 1990, www.ncbi.nlm.nih.gov/books/NBK286/, Abstract.

unusual growths, abnormal uterine bleeding, or other conditions[93], I thought I was going to pass out. Pain was so unbearable, I should have asked for a sedative beforehand.

Seemingly, the more I groaned, the more he kept repeating something like, *'Relax. It's only my fingers.'* Although wishing I was audacious enough to respond with, *'Now, tell me Doc. If the tables were turned, would you be relaxed if I shoved two fingers in your penis?'*, out of respect, I held my tongue until the fingering was over. Or, so I thought.

The butt-probing aspect of the exam was even more brutal. As I lay on my side, in went his finger and out went a couple of loud screams. Though familiar with digital rectal exams since I battled constipation for years, this time around, I just couldn't bear being poked with his sausage-size finger. In fact, it felt like I was being double-dipped.

Shortly after the exam, came the news. My doctor said, *"You have several large fibroids."*, at which point I began trembling in

---

[93] Long, WN. "Pelvic Examination." In: Walker, HK., Hall, WD., Hurst, JW., editors. Clinical Methods: The History, Physical, and Laboratory Examinations. 3rd edition. Chap. 177, Boston: Butterworths, 1990, www.ncbi.nlm.nih.gov/books/NBK286/, Abstract.

fear. Surely, I remembered a student mentioning the term after I had passed blood clots, for the first time, while teaching a computer class, at age 28. Thereafter, I recall reading only high-level information about fibroids considering I hadn't been diagnosed with having them. Other than that, I was clueless.

Sitting stupefied with *"What the heck are fibroids?"* swarming around in my head, I asked him to explain the condition in more detail. Responding with something similar to, *'Uterine fibroid tumors are growths of muscle and connective tissue in the uterus that are usually non-cancerous.'*, made me want to yank my cell phone out of my handbag and search the Internet for layperson explanations.

Instead of over the top medical jargon, I needed to understand what they were, why I had them, how long I had them, and how to get rid of them. Being an inopportune time for him to go into detail since he had other patients waiting to be seen, I left his office without fully knowing what I had just been diagnosed with. However, as soon as I returned home, I began researching all things fibroids.

Nicknamed *fireballs of the uterus* because they, generally, form in the shape of balls and can cause sheer havoc for some women, fibroids "*...also known as uterine myomas, leiomyomas, or fibromas, are firm, compact tumors that are made of smooth muscle cells and fibrous connective tissue that develop in the uterus*", according to The Yale Guide to Women's Reproductive Health: From Menarche to Menopause.[94] And, "*In more than 99 percent of fibroid cases, the tumors are benign (non-cancerous).*"[95]

Learning about the seven types of fibroids, that are named based on their location within the uterus, was head-spinning. Yet, I was determined to understand each type, so I'd have some idea as to what was dwelling inside my uterus and potentially causing overwhelming symptoms I had experienced for years.

"*Intramural fibroids grow within the muscular uterine wall (Latin, mur) and are extremely common.*" (Minkin 197)[96] If they become relatively large, intramural fibroids can make the uterus expand, significantly, and cause heavy menstrual flow and

---

[94] Minkin, MJ. and Wright, CV. "The Yale Guide to Women's Reproductive Health: From Menarche to Menopause." p. 195. The Yale University Press, 2008.
[95] "Fibroids: Symptoms, Treatment, Diagnosis." UCLA Obstetrics and Gynecology. 26 Mar. 2017. UCLA Health, www.obgyn.ucla.edu/fibroids.
[96] Minkin, MJ. and Wright, CV. "The Yale Guide to Women's Reproductive Health: From Menarche to Menopause." p. 197. The Yale University Press, 2008.

pressure.[97]

"Submucousal fibroids grow beneath the inner lining of the uterine cavity (called the mucosa), displacing it as they grow." (Minkin 197)[98] They *"...will often cause bleeding between periods and often cause severe cramping."*[99] And, *"Sometimes a submucousal fibroid develops a stalk, called a pedicle, which remains attached to the wall of the uterus while the fibroid itself may push into the uterine cavity"* (Minkin 197).[100] Referred to as *pedunculated fibroids, "Abrupt movements can cause penduncculated fibroids to rotate on these stems. This interrupts the blood flow to the fibroid, which can be extremely painful."*[101]

Intracavitary fibroids "...extend into the uterine cavity.", and

---

[97] Indman, PD. "Types of Uterine Fibroids." 19 Sep. 2011. *ObGYN.net*, www.obgyn.net/infertility/types-uterine-fibroids.
[98] Minkin, MJ. and Wright, CV. "The Yale Guide to Women's Reproductive Health: From Menarche to Menopause." p. 197. The Yale University Press, 2008.
[99] Indman, PD. "Types of Uterine Fibroids." 19 Sep. 2011. *ObGYN.net*, www.obgyn.net/infertility/types-uterine-fibroids.
[100] Minkin, MJ. and Wright, CV. "The Yale Guide to Women's Reproductive Health: From Menarche to Menopause." p. 197. The Yale University Press, 2008.
[101] "Uterine Fibroids: Overview." Informed Health Online [Internet]. Cologne, Germany: Institute for Quality and Efficiency in Health Care (IQWiG). 2006-. 22 Oct. 2014. Updated 16 Nov. 2017. www.ncbi.nlm.nih.gov/books/NBK279535/.

"can cause infertility."[102] They can also *"cause heavy bleeding."*[103] *"Subserousal fibroids grow on the outer wall of the uterus (called the serosa) and can push outward from the abdominal cavity"* (Minkin 197-198).[104] *"Since they are commonly larger than other types of fibroids, they can crowd into the uterus cavity and lead to heavy bleeding and other more serious complications."*[105]

"Interligamentous fibroids grow between the layers of the ligaments (the strong bands of connective tissue) that support the uterus inside the abdominal cavity" (Minkin 198).[106] And, *"Parasitic fibroids are fibroids with stalks that rest against another organ and attach to that organ, establishing a new blood supply"* (Minkin 198).[107]

In a nutshell, the adult uterus is shaped like an upturned

---

[102] "What to Do About Fibroids." Harvard Women's Health Watch. Jul. 2008. Harvard Health Publishing. Harvard Medical School, www.health.harvard.edu/womens-health/what_to_do_about_fibroids.

[103] "Fibroid FAQs." UCLA Obstetrics and Gynecology. 2018. UCLA Health, www.obgyn.ucla.edu/fibroid-faq.

[104] Minkin, MJ. and Wright, CV. "The Yale Guide to Women's Reproductive Health: From Menarche to Menopause." The Yale University Press, 2008.

[105] "Slideshow: A Visual Guide to Uterine Fibroids." 24 May 2018. Reviewed by Todd N., *WebMD*, www.webmd.com/women/uterine-fibroids/ss/slideshow-fibroid-overview.

[106] Minkin, MJ. and Wright, CV. "The Yale Guide to Women's Reproductive Health: From Menarche to Menopause." The Yale University Press, 2008.

[107] Minkin, MJ. and Wright, CV. "The Yale Guide to Women's Reproductive Health: From Menarche to Menopause." The Yale University Press, 2008.

pear and its length, width and thickness dimensions, respectively, *"...measures 7.5 cm x 4.5 cm x 3.0 cm in size and weighs approximately 60 g or 1 oz."*[108], according to Holland and Brews Manual of Obstetrics. Although the size of the uterus varies with each woman and can fluctuate based on several factors, a single fibroid can be microscopic or large enough to "*encompass the entire uterus.*"[109] The uterus can also contain multiple fibroid masses of varying sizes and weighing several pounds. In fact, *"...the largest, reported, fibroid ever recorded weighed in at 140 pounds."*[110]

Hearing the death knell when told I had fibroids and after researching the different types of fibroids, I assumed I was morgue bound. Not only was I suffering from PMS, PMDD, painful menstruation, heavy bleeding, anemia, chronic constipation, and frequent urination, I now had a *mass choir* of fibroids congregating

---

[108] Daftary, SN. and Chakravarti, S. "Holland And Brews Manual of Obstetrics." 3rd Ed., Chap. 1, p. 3. Elsevier Health Sciences, 2011.
[109] Cornforth, T. "Benign Uterine Fibroid Tumors Types and Treatments." 19 May 2018. Reviewed by Shur, M., *VeryWellHealth*, www.verywellhealth.com/benign-uterine-fibroid-tumors-3520704.
[110] Cornforth, T. "Benign Uterine Fibroid Tumors Types and Treatments." 19 May 2018. Reviewed by Shur, M., *VeryWellHealth*, www.verywellhealth.com/benign-uterine-fibroid-tumors-3520704.

inside my uterus.

Considering I underwent physicals practically every year, I was confounded that fibroids had gone undiagnosed. Furthermore, the likelihood of them originating as far back as when I first began passing blood clots, at age 28, made me feel like a victim of a medical conspiracy.

To confirm the diagnosis, my doctor ordered an ultrasound for the first time, at age 39. Also referred to as sonogram, the exam is, commonly, performed using either transabdominal (through the abdomen) or transvaginal (through the vagina) techniques that can detect fibroids and other conditions.[111]

Prior to the appointment, my doctor gave me a slip of paper with instructions to drink thirty-two ounces of liquid, two hours prior to the test. Since it stated, *'Any type of non-carbonated liquid will suffice'*, certainly, thirty-two ounces of Chardonnay would have worked wonders in taking the edge off my first ultrasound fears. But, on the other hand, it would have increased my chances of

---

[111] "Pelvic Ultrasound." Johns Hopkins Medicine. *Health Library*, www.hopkinsmedicine.org/healthlibrary/test_procedures/gynecology/pelvic_ultrasound_92,p07784.

being pulled over and issued a DUI for driving under the influence. Therefore, I drank what felt like gallons of water before arriving at the testing facility, to play it safe.

While signing in, the receptionist informed me that the ultrasound technician was running forty-five minutes late. She also advised that if I needed to use the restroom, I should empty only half of my bladder and replace the loss by drinking more water. To save myself public embarrassment for which I was accustomed having a frequent urination problem, I remained seated as spasms ricocheted throughout my bladder.

Approximately an hour later, the receptionist called my name. As I tottered into the exam room, I noticed the technician's unfriendly demeanor. After instructing me to unzip my pants, unbutton the lower half of my blouse, and lie on the exam table, he squirted a gel-like substance on my lower abdomen and pelvis and began passing the transducer probe over it.

Watching as he, repeatedly, shifted his eyes from my body to the monitor, I asked *"What are you seeing?"* to get an idea as to how many fibroid fiends were crammed inside my uterus. Without a response after asking twice, I felt like removing my pants and panties and squirting my thirty-two ounces of urine on him for not letting me know.

Once the transabdominal ultrasound was over, he mentioned divulging any information to patients could cost him his job. Though he should have disclosed such protocol as soon as I entered the exam room, I let it go as he was obviously having a bad morning—being late and all.

A week or so later, I received the ultrasound results which revealed, *"The uterus is markedly enlarged and measures 16 cm in length and 9.5 cm anteroposterior and 11.3 cm wide. There is markedly inhomogeneous parenchymal pattern with multiple hypoechoic uterine masses and demonstrates nodular uterine margin. There is central hyper echoic density 9.5 mm in thickness, which probably represents endometrial echo possible premenstrual proliferation. Ovarian echoes demonstrate no adnexal masses. No free cul de sac fluid can be detected. Impression: Multiple enlarged uterine fibroids."*

In explaining the size of my fibroids relative to fruit, vegetables and other objects by which they are commonly compared, my doctor mentioned my uterus was equivalent to that of a honeydew melon.[112] In *fetus speak*, it was larger than a four-month pregnancy!

Evidently, large and multiple fibroids were the culprit of many debilitating symptoms I had suffered, prior to and during my periods. They were the reason why menstruation felt as if a lit cherry bomb had been placed inside my vagina, even after popping pain pills and attaching either heating pads, wraps, or patches to my throbbing abdomen, pelvis and back to relieve pain. They were also the reason why blood clots as big as beefsteak tomatoes, braised beets, and rotten red potatoes stampeded out of me, regularly.

Dumbfounded, outraged and scared, I sought medical treatment opinions for my ballooning uterus and throng of symptoms. However, most doctors gave me the usual lip service such as *'Fibroids are normal and they usually shrink, so don't worry'*, and sent me on my miserable way with prescriptions for pain medication. Being the extent of treatment I received, I did as

---

[112] Parker, WH. "What Size are My Fibroids?" 4 Apr. 2013. Fibroids: A Gynecologist's Second Opinion. www.fibroidsecondopinion.com/2013/04/what-size-are-my-fibroids/.

was recommended for, approximately, three years.

With worsening symptoms, I returned to the doctor who initially diagnosed me with fibroids, at age 39. After performing a pelvic exam and feeling even larger fibroid masses, he ordered a complete blood count test and recommended that I undergo a second ultrasound to determine how rapid my fibroids were growing.

Preparing for the exam was similar to the first. However, when escorted into the exam room that had a humongous ultrasound machine and monitor, I was taken aback. I could only assume, the bigger the fibroids, the larger the imaging equipment. Thankfully, the ultrasound technician assured me that the equipment was just old and in need of an upgrade.

After placing gel on my abdomen and pelvis, he began probing away. As he kept staring at the monitor and pressing the button to capture images of my uterus, I nearly broke my neck trying to look at it. Though scared straight, I wanted to see what the creatures looked like. When I asked, *"What's the size of the largest one?"*, he stated, *"You have several large ones near your bladder and some are lodged within close proximity of your rectum."*

Although I regretted asking, his brief response helped confirm why I struggled with frequent urination and constipation for years. Apparently, fibroids were pressing against my bladder and rectum like paperweights.

When the second ultrasound report revealed, *"The uterus is very enlarged, with heterogeneous echogenicity. It measures 24 x 10 x 12 cm in size. Because of its enlarged size, the ovaries cannot be visualized. This is most consistent with a large leimyomatous uterus."*, I wanted to give up the ghost. My uterus had grown from the size of a honeydew melon to a cantaloupe and was now the size of a six-month pregnancy!

Just as devastating were the results of my complete blood count test that revealed my blood-iron level was 8 (normal range 45-180); hemoglobin 5.7 (normal range 11-16); hematocrit 19.9 (normal range 35-47); red blood count 3.34 (normal range 3.9-5.1); white blood count 7.2 (normal range 4-11); and platelets count 39 (normal 150-400).

Had ultrasound been ordered as soon as I expressed symptoms of a fibrous uterus, at age 28, and especially when they were smaller and treatable, I wouldn't have ended up with an enormous uterus, jammed-packed with fibroids. It's unfathomable that the disorder wasn't timely diagnosed considering the number of diagnostic methods available.

In addition to ultrasound, another technique called a *sonohystergram* or *saline infusion sonogram*, can accurately detect the location of intracavitary and intramural fibroids.[113] They can also be detected with *hysterosalpingogram (HSG)*, an X-ray using a dye that can visualize abnormal structures of the uterus and fallopian tubes and detect any distortion or enlargement of the uterus caused by fibroids and other conditions within the uterus.[114]

A procedure called *laparoscopy* views contents of the abdomen or pelvis using a long, thin telescope containing a bright light and camera called a *hysteroscope* that is inserted into a tiny incision made in or near the navel.[115] Likewise, fibroids can be detected by *hysteroscopy*, a procedure which inspects the uterus

---

[113] Bradley, L. "Menstrual Dysfunction." Aug. 2010. Cleveland Clinic. Center for Continuing Education. www.clevelandclinicmeded.com/medicalpubs/diseasemanagement/womens-health/menstrual-dysfunction/.

[114] "Hysterosalpingogram." *Infertility and Reproduction Guide,* 1 Apr. 2017. *WebMD.com*, www.webmd.com/infertility-and-reproduction/guide/hysterosalpingogram-21590#1.

[115] "Diagnostic Laparoscopy." 24 May 2016. *MedlinePlus*, www.medlineplus.gov/ency/article/003918.htm.

and examines the uterine lining, organs and structures within the uterus using a fine hysteroscope to accurately diagnose fibroids and other conditions.[116]

Additionally, fibroids can be confirmed through *magnetic resonance imaging (MRI)*, an imaging technology which provides quality images of the uterus as well as the exact number and location of fibroids using magnets and radio waves.[117] They can also be detected through *computed tomography* or *CT Scan* which is a two-part imaging technology using a combination of X-ray views taken from different angles and computer processing to pinpoint the exact location of fibroids.[118]

Having a village of vile vagrants perched inside my womb, it's no wonder I was often asked if I was pregnant. Had I courage to nip each inquiry in the bud, I would have said, *"Yes, I'm a*

---

[116] Bradley, L. "Menstrual Dysfunction." Aug. 2010. Cleveland Clinic. Center for Continuing Education. www.clevelandclinicmeded.com/medicalpubs/diseasemanagement/womens-health/menstrual-dysfunction/.

[117] "Fibroid Treatment Program." UCLA Obstetrics and Gynecology. 1 Apr. 2017. UCLA Health, www.obgyn.ucla.edu/fibroid-faq.

[118] "What is Computed Tomography?" 23 Apr. 2014. U.S. Department of Health and Human Services. *U.S. Food and Drug Administration*, www.fda.gov/Radiation-EmittingProducts/RadiationEmittingProductsandProcedures/MedicalImaging/MedicalX-Rays/ucm115318.htm.

whopping 24-weeks pregnant with what's called uterine fibroid tumors, a disease of unknown cause. They are muscle masses and connective tissue similar to the look and feel of cow guts, that mysteriously form and grow in the uteruses of 1 in 4 women in the United States.[119] *In addition to causing uterus-in-the-mouth-of-JAWS type of pain, prior to and during menstruation, the disorder makes my abdomen swell to the size of a pumpkin. So, now that you have a hunch, I am not 'with child'. I am 'with ferocious fibroids' and pray that I'll be delivered from them someday!"*

Often feeling like the *"woman with an issue of blood"*[120], in Mark 5:25-34 of the Bible, I too had faith and believed prayer would set me free. Morning, noon and night, I'd drop to my knees and pray the Lord's Prayer. Thereafter, I'd pray from the heart and say, *"Lord, I'm begging for your grace and mercy. And, I pray that my works in life, thus far, are worthy of a miracle in curing fibroid tumors that are rapidly growing inside me and causing me to bleed heavily and experience many other horrible symptoms which*

---

119 Luckstein, K. "Exploring Treatment Options for Women with Fibroids." Mayo Clinic, 23 Apr. 2015, www.newsnetwork.mayoclinic.org/discussion/exploring-treatment-options-for-women-with-fibroids/.
120 The Bible. Authorized King James Version, Oxford University Press, 1998.

neither my doctors nor I can do anything about. Dear God, please hear my cries as I humbly beg you to please, please, please remove this sickness from me. In Jesus name, I'll always pray. Amen."

Sex and Sheer Suffering

Prior to the invasion of fibroids, my sex life was great. But, with colonies of fibroids residing in my uterus, sexual intercourse felt like I was being gangbanged by sadomasochistic horses. Often causing me to wail as if my hymen were still intact, it's no wonder the few men in my life assumed I was having emotional meltdowns during sex.

Fibroids destroyed every aspect of intimacy. Whenever pleasure from sensual massage or other act of foreplay heightened, I would either downplay excitement or evade intimate advances entirely. Knowing imminent intercourse was bound to feel as if a stretch limousine had reeled inside me and impede my ability to reach the *Big O* or any level of orgasmic bliss, oftentimes, I'd *just say no to sex* as I would to drugs.

Having intercourse, a day or two before my periods, was most unpleasant. Initially, slow movement and cautious prodding felt like I didn't have any fibroids at all. However, as excitement peaked and pounding began, pain felt as if fibroids were banging against my cervix that would cause my entire body to spasm. With my vocal chords being the only part unscathed, I'd often cry at the pitch of a colicky newborn while being ridden as fast as a car on a German autobahn. Not only would I stiffen like a cadaver throughout, the dreadful episodes usually triggered early onset of my periods.

I remember fearing intercourse, outercourse, and all else with my boyfriend, one evening, especially after feeling huge bumps protruding from my lower abdomen and pelvis. With my period being two days away and fibroids lying in wait for blood to flow so they could feed like crazy, I knew penetrative sex would result in, yet, another unbearable and unfulfilling encounter—for us both.

Experiencing an array of agonizing premenstrual symptoms with fibroids kicking my uterus, cervix and butt too, my boyfriend drew an aromatherapy bath to help put me out of misery, that evening. As I laid immersed in the warm, scented tub for forty-five minutes or so, most symptoms subsided. Therefore, I stepped out the tub, dried myself, and popped a painkiller just in case he wanted me to return the favor.

Seeing rose petals on the bed and a beautiful bouquet of long-stemmed, multi-colored roses on the nightstand brought a huge smile to my face. Apparently, he darted to the store to get them while I was in the tub. Being the most romantic man, I had ever dated, he would regularly shower me with flowers, chocolate, poems, and all else. However, he had never gone this far in creating such a sensual environment.

As foreplay escalated, I hopped on top of him as excited as a frisky, unspayed cat. But, as soon as penetration began, my vagina felt like it had split in two. Seemingly, the pain pill I had taken prior exited with my bodily secretions as I rocked forward and backward, as rigid as a surf board.

Aware of my battle with fibroids, although it took over a year to share the disorder with him, he was usually gentle and would repeatedly ask if I was comfortable. However, the moment thrusting ensued, intercourse felt like a scud missile had detonated inside my vagina. Launching into glass-breaking screams as if fibroids were being rammed inside the crevices of my brain, I'm surprised I never fell unconscious during the spine-bending ordeals.

To accommodate my hell-raising fibroids and make intercourse less deplorable, we regularly discussed positions which felt more tolerable than others. We also agreed to only have intercourse a week before the premenstrual phases of my cycles and after my periods ended. Engaging in sex during menstruation was out of the question, as that week was reserved for *fibroid feasting*. However, all the scheduling and experimentation with positions, in the world, could neither control when we had sex nor prevent pain.

After several more bedroom disasters, I sensed he was as fed up with fibroids as myself. Though he seemed sympathetic towards my plight, he expressed that he could no longer deal with my *non-engagement* during sex. Knowing that I experienced more pain than pleasure and would, oftentimes, go through the motions with the end in mind, he ended our four-year relationship.

Apparently, having a uterus full of fibroids and roster of horrendous symptoms was a major turn-off. With no control over the disorder, it was impossible to maintain relationships. Yet, I was determined to prevent fibroids from ruining intimacy and formed a companionship with a *well-endowed* man, a few years later.

Although tempted to double-dose on pain medication prior to each sexual encounter, I feared developing stomach bleeding or ending up in the emergency room. Therefore, whenever we had intercourse, I endured pain which felt as if fibroids were being pierced through all three layers of my uterine wall. Often requesting *time out* not only killed most intimate moments, it eventually killed the relationship too.

In the heat of passion, some women patiently wait for men to *get it up*. I, on the other hand, impatiently waited for them to get the darn thing out. Unable to sustain relationships because of fibroids, I searched endlessly for information on why intercourse caused such ripping pain and how to enjoy sexual intercourse with large fibroids. Finding little made me feel like I was the only woman dealing with this issue, naturally. However, stumbling across a disorder called *dyspareunia*, *"recurrent or persistent genital pain before, during or after sexual intercourse"*[121], gave me some incite.

While symptoms of dyspareunia may have both physical and psychological origins[122], I focused solely on physical reasons

---

[121] "Painful Intercourse (Dyspareunia)." 12 Jan. 2018. Mayo Clinic, www.mayoclinic.org/diseases-conditions/painful-intercourse/symptoms-causes/syc-20375967.

[122] "Painful Intercourse (Dyspareunia)." 12 Jan. 2018. Mayo Clinic, www.mayoclinic.org/diseases-conditions/painful-intercourse/symptoms-causes/syc-20375967.

since I had never been emotionally traumatized by anything other than fibroids. Learning that dyspareunia may be caused by certain conditions such as uterine fibroid tumors, I explored several self-help remedies such as using lubricant, changing coital positions, engaging in longer foreplay, and performing vaginal relaxation and deep breathing exercises. But, regardless of all that I did to minimize pain, intercourse still felt as if I was being socked in the vagina.

I never forget being terrified of starting a sexual relationship with a man I had known for over two years. Initially having a platonic one that neither of us wanted to ruin, we were reluctant in taking our relationship to the next level. I was hesitant even more so, as I didn't want to go through the disappointment in having little satisfaction in the sack and eventually chasing him away—like all the others.

However, unable to resist sexual tension between us, one evening, I called upon all the remedies and techniques I had researched so intercourse wouldn't be as painful. As we took our time cuddling and engaging in foreplay, I felt somewhat at ease even though my period was due any moment. But, as soon as penetration began, it felt as if my vaginal innards were headed toward the North Pole.

Vaulting out of bed to avoid staining my bedsheet and him too, I cupped my throbbing crotch and limped to the bathroom. After taking a long shower, I stuck a footlong sanitary napkin in the center of my thong and tottered back to bed. Thankfully, he wasn't awake to see me in all my unsexy glory.

Another disastrous encounter occurred when we were *going at it* on a cream-colored sectional I had purchased a few days prior. Noticing bloodstains on it, he said something like, *'Don't worry, these things happen.'* Embracing me for several minutes as I cried from both pain and embarrassment, he then rushed to the kitchen to search for upholstery cleaning supplies and I raced to the bathroom to prevent staining the carpet too.

With fibroids ruining the majority of my relationships, surely, I wished my body would combust so all of the blood-sucking, sex-deterring masses would somehow fall out of me and drop dead. Welcoming themselves into the bedroom and destroying every possibility of pleasure, inevitably, placed a damper on my sex life. Instead of *making love*, I usually focused on *making pain go away*.

And, as a result, I dated little during the 15 years of living with fibroids.

While most men I dated were genuinely concerned about my disorder and preoccupation with pain, some would inquire about the drastic changes in the size of my abdomen that appeared as flat as a pancake after my periods ended but would grow to the size of a six-month pregnancy, prior to and during my cycles. Though my explanation that fibroids caused my stomach to protrude seemed digestible, whenever such conversations triggered questions as to whether I could have children with so many fibroids in my uterus, I knew the relationships were doomed.

In addition to making it impossible to have a quality sex life and causing an overwhelming sense of sexual inadequacy, fibroids lowered my self-esteem and confidence. Compelled to either engage in painful intercourse to maintain some level of sexual competence or refrain from it entirely was so tormenting, I began losing interest in sex.

Prior to chaos-causing fibroids, I had more self-esteem and confidence than I could handle. However, as they grew out of control such attributes were replaced with fear and anxiety.

Stripping away my desire for intimacy, fibroids also made me feel disempowered and insecure. Even my self-image nosedived considering my disfigured abdomen and pelvis would swell for several days each month.

Fearing relationships and having a dwindling sex drive, body image, and so much more, prompted me seek help. Once urinary tract infection, vaginal dryness, vaginismus, vestibulodynia, vulvodynia, and every other female condition beginning with the letter 'V' were ruled out, I was told that I may have estrogen dominance. Since fibroids are hypersensitive to estrogen[123], I needed to balance my disproportionate levels of estrogen, relative to progesterone, in order to regain and maintain a healthy sex drive.

Suggesting I take a natural approach by eating insoluble fiber that binds to estrogen and keeps the body from absorbing too much of it, I ate oats, wheat bran, apples, cauliflower, beans, and other sources of insoluble fiber. However, they did nothing more

---

[123] McWilliams, MM. and Chennathukuzhi, VM. "Recent Advances in Uterine Fibroid Etiology." *Semin Reprod Med*, 9 Mar. 2017, Vol. 35, no. 2, pp. 181-189, doi:10.1055/s-0037-1599090, Abstract.

than cause gas and diarrhea. Also recommending that I either increase the dose of pain medication prior to intercourse or abstain from sex entirely, I chose the latter and my libido remained out of service like an unpaid cell phone bill.

Watchfully Waiting for What?

During the three-year period, between my first and second ultrasounds, I was told to *watch and wait*. Although a common approach in monitoring fibroids so health care providers can recommend the best course of treatment, I later learned, *"Expectant management or watchful waiting is suitable for patients with asymptomatic or mildly symptomatic fibroids."*[124]

To the contrary, I had symptomatic fibroids that needed immediate medical intervention as opposed to watchfully waiting for them to kill me! It was bad enough that I was officially diagnosed with the disorder many years after they had acquired the deed to my uterus. Yet, I had to trust that doctors knew best in recommending expectant management and my fibroids would either shrink or disappear, eventually.

While sitting on the sidelines with fibroids growing out of control and symptoms worsening, I continued experimenting with alternative therapies hoping to minimize them. I also switched back

---

[124] Wu, H-H. and Wang, L. "Gunner Goggles Obstetrics and Gynecology." p. 73, Elsevier, 2018.

to a vegan diet, avoiding red meat, dairy, soy, and other food that's said to trigger fibroid growth. However, treating the many debilitating symptoms was virtually impossible.

The psychological effects of symptomatic, uterine fibroid tumors were just as overwhelming as the physical symptoms. In fact, researchers have found that women had, *"Significant emotional response to their fibroids, ranging from general worry and concern to fear, anxiety, sadness, and depression."*[125], based on the results of a survey given to forty-eight women who were diagnosed with symptomatic fibroids.

Evidently, I wasn't the only one feeling helpless and hopeless as I moaned, groaned, and moved about the planet with a uterus congested to the hilt with fibroids. I remember being bed-ridden over an entire weekend as I battled a barrage of fibroid-induced symptoms and premenstrual madness. Engulfed in uncontainable emotions, all I could think about was my bloody, pain-riddled, hapless reality. Though I tried stamping out negative

---

[125] Ghant, MS., Lawson AK., et al. "Beyond the Physical: A Qualitative Assessment of the Emotional Burden of Symptomatic Uterine Fibroids on Women's Mental Health." *Fertility and Sterility*, 21 Oct. 2014, Vol. 102, no. 3, ed. 248, doi.org/10.1016/j.fertnstert.2014.07.844, Abstract.

thoughts by reading and journaling, I felt overwhelmingly depressed about not having any control over fibroids and consumed with feelings of isolation. Drowning in tears and indulging in the piteous of parties, I had to wait until the dark clouds lifted at the tail end of the weekend. Then, my period began.

Another instance in which made clear that fibroids had taken its toll on my emotional well-being occurred in my early 40s. I remember contorting in cramping pain so severe, I felt like my abdomen and pelvis were being bashed with a crowbar. Roaming, aimlessly, in circles as I waited for medication to ease pain, surely, the thought of reaching for a steak knife to put me out of misery sooner crossed my mind. Instead, I hit the floor in attempt to stabilize pain since lying in bed or on the couch usually caused pain to worsen.

Although accustomed to seeing huge lumps protrude from my abdomen a few days before my periods, lifting my head to steal a glance, this particular time, scared me to tears. My grossly distorted abdomen looked as if it were filled beyond capacity with a bunch of bald, baby wombats. Turning my head left and right to view it from different angles, I lay horrorstruck by the sight.

As I delicately touched the hard, bulging bumps with my fingers and felt them inch into vacant spaces of my clogged uterus, I thought I was hallucinating. Trying my best not to succumb to heightening anxiety, even though my *traveling fibroids* the size of lemons, oranges and avocadoes were sashaying around in my uterus, I rose and readied myself for a trip to the emergency room.

However, echoing responses I had received from health care providers that were on par with, *'Yes, you'll feel lumps in your abdomen as fibroids grow. However, feeling lumps is better than having an unnecessary procedure. So, let's continue monitoring any new growth spurts and symptoms by watching and waiting.'*, stopped me dead in my tracks. Assuming I'd hear the same thing had I gone to the emergency room, I resumed lying on the floor while staring at my grotesque abdomen in utter fear and disgust.

Oftentimes, I'd ask myself, *"Why am I watching and waiting as my life is being turned upside down by rapidly growing fibroids and atrocious symptoms? Am I chasing waterfalls believing my large fibroids will either shrink or disappear? Am I playing Russian roulette with my life without knowing how grave the game? And, are there other women, in my family, who've dealt with or are currently dealing with symptomatic, uterine fibroid tumors?"*

While I felt comfortable discussing most things with my mother, shame and embarrassment prevented me from talking about fibroids, menstruation-related woes, and all else pertaining to the *downstairs department.* However, when diagnosed with full-blown fibroids and told to watch and wait, I finally confided in her.

The moment I shared my horrors, not only did she reveal that she too battled fibroids for over ten years, she mentioned her symptoms had become so incapacitating that she was forced to have a hysterectomy in her early 40s. Revealing my uterus was the size of a four-month pregnancy, after the first ultrasound, she was shocked. And, as she shared her dreadful experiences living with fibroids, I was shocked. Seemingly, our symptoms including heavy bleeding, painful menstruation, anemia, constipation, frequent urination were practically identical.

With my *"I have fibroids"* announcement birthing subsequent conversations surrounding what seemed like a *generational secret*, I learned that several women in my family had uteruses infested with fibroids. Hearing her say something similar to, *'So-and-so also had them and needed to undergo a second surgical procedure to remove grapefruit-size fibroids because they had grown back larger than before.'* And, *'Many had symptoms so debilitating, they also had hysterectomies in their early 40s'*, was not only eye-opening, it confirmed I was not alone.

Divulging my disorder to my mother made me realize just how injurious fear, shame and embarrassment can be. Instead of shrouding in secrecy, it's important to communicate openly about fibroids and all other female-related disorders. Had I known fibroids ran in my family, I may have prevented years of long-suffering and avoided going at fibroids alone. I may have also been much more assertive in requesting that health care providers do more than recommend that I take birth control pills, pain medication, and watch and wait.

While researchers can't put a finger on what causes fibroids, many suspicions have been raised as to what increases a woman's chance of developing them. According to researchers at the National Institute of Child Health and Human Development and the University of South Florida, Tampa who conducted the largest screening of fibroids in the United States in 2002, heredity is suspected in increasing the risk of developing fibroid tumors.[126]

Other studies have shown that obesity is a risk factor for fibroids However, a 2008 study published in the Proceedings of the National Academy of Sciences *(PNAS)* shows, "*Growth rates were not influenced by tumor size, location, body mass index, or parity.*"[127]

Research has linked estrogen to fibroids. According to an online article published by UCLA Obstetrics and Gynecology, *"While it is not clearly known what causes fibroids, it is believed that each tumor develops from an aberrant muscle cell in the uterus, which multiplies rapidly because of the influence of estrogen."*[128]

Regrettably, watching and waiting afforded ample time for fibroids to grow to such enormous sizes, my candidacy for most fibroid shrinkage and removal procedures dwindled. Learning such

---

[126] Tsibris, JCM., Segars, J., et al. "Insights from Gene Arrays on the Development and Growth Regulation of Uterine Leiomyomata." *Fertility and Sterility*, 2002, Vol. 78, no. 1, pp. 114-121, doi.org/10.1016/S0015-0282(02)03191-6, Abstract.

[127] Peddada, SD., Laughlin, SK., et al. "Growth of Uterine Leiomyomata Among Premenopausal Black and White Women." *PNAS,* 16 Dec. 2008, Vol. 105, no. 50, pp. 19887-19892, doi:10.1073/pnas.0808188105, Abstract.

[128] "Fibroids: Symptoms, Treatment, Diagnosis." UCLA Obstetrics and Gynecology. 26 Mar. 2017. UCLA Health, www.obgyn.ucla.edu/fibroids.

an approach should only be recommended when fibroids are relatively small and cause little to no symptoms was infuriating. Had I known watching and waiting would result in fibroids growing even larger, naturally, I would have sought surgical intervention sooner.

Seeking medical attention was as distressing as receiving morbid results of the second ultrasound. The first consultation was with a gynecologist whom my primary care physician had referred. While reviewing a copy of my recent ultrasound report, I shared that I had researched her background, areas of expertise, and affiliations with various hospitals. I also mentioned how impressed I was by the different types of fibroid surgeries she regularly performed.

Then, I explained why I preferred *myomectomy*, a minimally invasive procedure involving *"…the removal of fibroids (non-cancerous tumors) from the wall of the uterus.*"[129], with understanding that fibroids can grow back after this type of surgery. And, as I rambled on about my desire to have children down the

---

[129] "Myomectomy." The Gale Encyclopedia of Surgery and Medical Tests. 7 Nov. 2018. *Encyclopedia.com*, www.encyclopedia.com/medicine/divisions-diagnostics-and-procedures/medicine/myomectomy.

line, she, abruptly, stated that I needed an emergency hysterectomy.

Without a smidgen of compassion, she mentioned that if I were to undergo such surgery, I would likely die from major blood loss. Adding insult to injury, she proceeded in telling me that I was "*too old*" to have children and would risk either miscarrying or having an unhealthy child. Then, in a pushy, saleswoman-like manner, she informed me that my best bet was hysterectomy.

Warning that I act immediately, she glanced at her calendar and offered available dates for surgery. Giving me two options that were three months in advance, made me question why she deemed it an emergency hysterectomy. Therefore, having a bad taste in my mouth once the consultation was over, I placed the intake forms I had completed in my handbag, so the *crook* wouldn't bill my insurance company, illegally, and stormed out of her office. Unnerved about her emergency hysterectomy recommendation and perturbed by her horrible disposition and blatant sales tactics, I drove home both tearful and stewing with agitation.

The next day, I saw my primary care physician to share what had transpired. Shocked that I walked out on the doctor whom he referred, I explained that her hysterectomy suggestion scared the crap out of me. In response, he gave me another referral and recommended that I schedule an appointment right away. In providing referral information, he mentioned the doctor was an oncologist! In asking if my fibroids were cancerous, he said something like, *'I don't believe so, but the oncologist will perform tests to find out for sure.'*

Fearing they were and refusing to see the *cancer doctor*, I took to the Internet searching high and low for a solution. Using a series of keywords from *fibroids are about to kill me* to *how to get rid of fibroids without surgery*, I spent hours viewing websites containing information that ranged from miracle remedies touting to either shrink or make fibroids disappear within days to robotic fibroid removal procedures—and everything in between.

Stumbling upon *gonadotropin-releasing hormone agonists* or *GnRHa*, a drug that blocks the master reproductive hormone; shuts down the body's ability to produce estrogen and progesterone; and causes fibroids to shrink[130], I felt like I had won the lottery. Elated to find treatment that would shrink fibroids and make most symptoms go away, I immediately began searching for doctors who administered the drug. And, after reviewing several profiles, I scheduled an appointment with a doctor who both administered GnRHa and specialized in the myomectomy procedure.

During the consultation, she performed a pelvic exam even though I had given her a copy of my recent ultrasound report. When asked if I was a good candidate for myomectomy, she responded with something similar to, *'Considering the size of your uterus, if you were to undergo a myomectomy you will, undoubtedly, experience massive blood loss. Additionally, there would be little left of your uterus to stitch back together after removing the fibroids.'*

Being denied the myomectomy procedure a second time was devastating. As she tried to convince me that my uterus

---

130 Hackenberg, R., Gesenhues, T., et al. "The Response of Uterine Fibroids to GnRH-Agonist Treatment Can be Predicted in Most Cases After One Month." *Eur J Obstet Gynecol Reprod Biol*, 3 Jul. 1992, Vol. 45, no. 2, pp. 125-129, doi.org/10.1016/0028-2243(92)90228-Q, Abstract.

needed to be removed if I wanted to regain my quality of life, I presumed she had lost her mind. Unsure as to whether she was looking out for my best interests or giving me the usual *hysterectomy sales pitch*, I had to assume the latter since I, repeatedly, told her that I didn't want my uterus removed.

After insisting upon a GnRHa injection which would shrink my fibroids in preparation for hysterectomy and temporarily put me out of misery, she scheduled the procedure. While she may have thought she had *sold* a hysterectomy that day, little did she know I was aware of what I called the *hysterectomy game*. Therefore, after receiving the shot, I forked over an outlandish amount of money, walked out of her office, and never returned. Neither did I call the next day, as promised, to confirm my availability to have my uterus amputated.

Although I enjoyed the three-month breather from my horrendous periods, I experienced hot flashes and insomnia that were likely due to a dramatic drop in estrogen levels. And, fibroids that may have shrank returned to their hefty sizes as did incapacitating symptoms.

Therefore, back to the drawing board I went in finding

treatment that would rid my body of fibroids, yet, preserve my uterus. Befriending a woman at a company in which I consulted, she mentioned a procedure called *uterine fibroid embolization* or *UFE*, a minimally invasive procedure that *"...involves the catheterization of both uterine arteries and the installation of tiny micro particles of polyvinyl alcohol."*[131]

Believing my prayers had been answered, I excitedly sat an appointment. In setting foot inside the doctor's office, I thought I had died and gone to heaven as the upscale medical facility was so posh, it resembled an interior design showroom. And, after filling out an exorbitant number of forms that took nearly an hour to complete, I was seen by the doctor.

First, he asked several questions regarding my health, then he discussed the pros and cons of various types of fibroid treatment. Knowing I wasn't a good candidate for most procedures, I patiently sat listening to his twenty-minute spiel. Handing me several pamphlets to further persuade me that UFE was the best

---

[131] Goodwin, SC. and Walker, WJ. "Uterine Artery Embolization for the Treatment of Uterine Fibroids." *Curr Opin Obstet Gynecol*, Sep. 1998, Vol. 10, no. 4, pp. 315-320, doi:10.1097/00001703-199808000-00006, Abstract.

treatment for my large and multiple fibroids, made me feel like I was sitting in front of a used car salesman—not a doctor. He, then, asked about my income and informed me that I'd have to pay out of pocket since most insurance companies won't pay for the UFE procedure.

Advising that he needed to perform a pelvic exam, I mentioned that I'd undergone three of them within the past month or so. However, he insisted I have another in case my fibroids had grown since the last exam. While his request didn't make any sense to me, I went along with it as the procedure would preserve my uterus in the event I wanted to have children in the future.

After performing the pelvic exam and reviewing my ultrasound reports, he told me I needed to have an *emergency UFE*—that same day. Claiming my fibroids were the largest he'd ever seen and blood counts were critically low, he scheduled an appointment for me to, first, see a hematologist to increase them. He, then, instructed the intake assistant to schedule a van to transport me to the hospital because I was *'too sick'* to drive, as he inferred.

With constant pressure to sign consent forms, I was

frightened and didn't know what to do. Asking to use the phone to call my mother in New York, the intake assistant escorted me inside a small room and sat as I tearfully regurgitated all the doctor had said. As she placed a pile of forms under my nose and gestured that I sign them so they could be faxed over to the hospital, I ended the call with my mother and thought, *"Okay, I've had enough!"*

Apparently, the doctor, the intake assistant, and staff were all in cahoots. Their scare tactics were not only nerve-wracking, they were outlandish and obviously orchestrated. Therefore, I told the doctor and his gang, *"Thanks, but no thanks"* and walked out. A few weeks later, I received a bill for over two thousand dollars for the two-hour visit.

Undoubtedly, the medical business is run like show business, I thought. Just as entertainers are considered commodities, my fibroid-filled uterus was a hot one. Though I felt as if I'd been thrown to the wolves, I was determined to find an honest and compassionate medical professional who could remove my large fibroids while retaining my ability to conceive.

A few days after the UFE fiasco, I somehow gained the courage to see the oncologist whom my family care physician had referred. During the consultation, I asked if my fibroids were cancerous and he stated that he needed to run tests first. I then shared that I'd only entertain conversations pertaining the myomectomy procedure as he looked at me as if I were nuts—considering my uterus was the size of a six-month pregnancy.

As mentioned by other doctors I had seen, he too insisted that I'd unlikely live through the surgery because of the sizes of my fibroids. And, in asking which type of procedure would be best, at this stage, he stated that he needed to perform a pelvic exam to gain a better sense as to the size and condition of my uterus. Though I had given him copies of recent pelvic exams and ultrasound reports as well as informed him that I was on the second day of my period, he still requested that I undergo another pelvic exam.

Having as many pelvic exams as I did, I could've performed one on myself. In mentioning that he also needed to draw blood, I flipped out knowing I had little blood in my body based on my blood test results and was losing even more during the appointment.

Even with my uncontrollable emotions, he remained professional as he delicately explained that the only way he could determine if my fibroids were cancerous and recommend the best type of treatment was to perform the exam. And, after instructing me to undress and put on the exam gown, he left the exam room.

A nervous wreck and overwhelmed by all the testing, results, and medical opinions, I sat on the exam table bawling my eyes out. When he returned, I began blurting out how sick and tired I was of pelvic exams and couldn't bear having another. Before he could process and respond to my rants, I dashed past him, rushed out his office, and never returned.

CHAPTER 5
Simon Says…Surgery!

ER and East-Wing Experiences

February 1, 2009 is a date forever etched in my mind. That evening, my next-door neighbor with whom I had developed a friendship stopped by. Sitting at my desk, we talked about our careers, relationships, and seemingly everything under the sun. With similar interests in website design and software application development, we brainstormed several ideas and discussed forming a joint venture.

Less than an hour into our conversation, I was overcome by the worst menstrual cramping pain I'd ever experienced. I also felt extremely weak from having bled more than thirty days straight after taking birth control pills containing synthetic progesterone called *drospirenone*[132]. Though recommended by a doctor who vowed they would control my heavy bleeding and hinder fibroid growth, I'd recently stopped taking them, as advised.

Crossing my legs and trying my best not to grimace, we continued chitchatting. But, as soon as I began flooding, an hour or

---

[132] "Drospirenone and Ethinyl Estradiol (Oral Route)." 1 Oct. 2018. *Mayo Clinic*, www.mayoclinic.org/drugs-supplements/drospirenone-and-ethinyl-estradiol-oral-route/description/drg-20061917.

so later, I felt like I was about to die smack dab in front of my neighbor. With blood clots piercing through my uterus and blasting out of my vagina, the thought of excusing myself to use the bathroom wasn't an option. Had I stood, blood and clots would've plopped onto the carpet and everything else. Therefore, to avoid the embarrassment of him seeing me drenched, I remained seated as blood matter flooded the two maternity pads I had worn.

Mentioning he had to make a few calls, I asked him to close the door and I'd lock it behind him. As I sat in what felt like a sea of blood and clots, I contemplated whether I should head to the bathroom, first, or lock the door. Deciding the latter was more important, I placed my right hand on the desk to raise myself from the chair. Cupping my left hand under my crotch, I limped to the door as blood continued barging out of me.

As I headed toward the bathroom, pain began ricocheting throughout my abdomen and pelvis so violently, I couldn't make it past the kitchen. Grasping onto the sink as I began breathing rapidly and my face, fingers and feet started tingling, I assumed I was hyperventilating and rummaged through the broom closet in search of a bag to breathe in to. However, in seeing blood clots the size of plums and pomegranates streaming down my legs and hitting the linoleum, I collapsed onto the kitchen floor.

Awakening to my dog's yelps and nudges on my forehead while clueless as to how long I was lying blacked out, it took several minutes to register what had happened. As he gazed into my eyes with a concerning look, I began crying aloud. Clearly, he knew something was wrong and was bent on reviving me by licking my tears away, as the nub of his tail wagged uncontrollably.

Without strength to stand, I crawled to the bathroom located inside my bedroom. After removing my bloodied, clot-riddled maternity pads, I sat on the toilet praying for dear life. Thereafter, I cleaned myself up, changed clothes, and headed to the emergency room.

Prior to getting in my car, I knocked on my neighbor's door to let him know where I was going. In asking, *"What's wrong?"*, I responded with something like, *"I have a female problem I need to have checked out. That's all."* While I should have mentioned that I was bleeding heavily and had collapsed shortly after he left, shame and embarrassment prevented me from doing so—even during my scariest and darkest hour.

However, when I arrived at the emergency room, I was compelled to inform the intake specialist of all that had happened and my long history with fibroids. I also mentioned that I had recently stopped taking birth control pills that may have caused me to bleed thirty consecutive days. And, as soon as I gave her the name and approximate date in which I started taking them, a medical bracelet was placed on my wrist. I was, then, rushed inside a curtained room where my vitals were taken and a blood test administered by an ER technician.

Still bleeding, clotting and cramping like crazy, I asked the technician for maternity pads. Those I had on were buckling likely due to the tight-fitting adult diaper I had worn for added protection. As I waited for him to return, an ultrasound technician and her assistant appeared with several long and wide pads, instead. After briefly introducing themselves, they helped me into a wheelchair which I thought was odd and wheeled me inside an examination room.

I was, then, asked to remove my skirt and panties. As I lay on the exam table, the assistant removed my sanitary paraphernalia and placed a large cotton pad underneath me, which

I also thought was strange. Feeling like a soiled newborn instead of a forty-three-year-old was most humbling. I was so humiliated that I'm surprised I didn't run, bottomless, out of the emergency room—leaving a trail of blood and clots in my path.

The ultrasound technician, then, mentioned that the doctor had ordered a *transvaginal ultrasound* to examine my pelvic organs and sizes of my fibroids. Since I only had transabdominal ultrasounds in the past, I was frightened of the vaginal method, especially because I was bleeding up a storm and cramping to no end. Thankfully, they were female with friendly demeanors which made me feel more at ease. However, as soon as the technician placed a condom-covered probe inside my vagina, I had nothing but malice toward them both.

Cringing in pain from what felt like a body massager prodding my uterus, cervix, ovaries and every other organ, I thought my vagina was going to explode. Spasms were so excruciating, I requested that the ultrasound technician remove it twice. After replacing the condom for the third time, she recommended that I insert the probe myself. Speechless and trying my best to disguise the look of utter disgust on my face, I politely said, *"Thanks for asking, but if I were to do it, you'd likely have to resuscitate me."*

Prior to the third attempt, she insisted the intensity of pain would lessen if I relaxed. As she further tried convincing me that the width of the wand was equivalent to a super-size tampon and most women feel little pain during vaginal ultrasound, I nearly went ballistic. What she failed to realize was that the wand was not only striking my enlarged, fibroid-filled uterus, blood clots were also being rammed against it—which hurt like hell.

As she resumed pressing on my abdomen while simultaneously moving the probe inside me, it felt like I was being socked in the vagina. However, the more I relaxed, the more my body seemed to adjust to the *foreign object*.

With tears lessening and tension lifting, I was then curious to know why they were staring at the monitor. Jokingly asking, *"Are the aliens now the size of pumpkin?"*, knowing sonographers aren't allowed to divulge information to patients, I'd hope they'd respond. Instead, their eyes remained transfixed as if they were viewing something of the extraterrestrial kind. Minutes later, the ultrasound technician whispered, *"All I can say is that you have the oddest-*

shaped uterus I have ever seen!"

Being well aware of my misshapen uterus, I told them that stealing a glance at the monitor from previous ultrasounds showed some fibroids were attached to stalks which meant I had pedunculated fibroids. And, every time the stem-like structures would *twist and shout*, sharp shooting pain would bring me to my knees.

Why sonographers aren't allowed to share what they see on the monitor with patients with fibroids, as they do with pregnant women, boggled my mind. Since I was virtually *pregnant with fibroids*, I should've at least been informed as to where their ugly heads and stalks were located in my uterus. While I understand sonographers aren't doctors and can't make diagnoses, offering me some information is the least they can do, especially after sticking a giant probe inside my vagina.

Once the *wicked wand* was removed, afterpain warranted vaginal physical therapy to recover from the maddening exam. Adding insult to injury, the technician informed me that I going to be admitted into the hospital. When I asked, *"For how long?"*, she said, *"I really can't say, but it may be awhile."*, as she placed a second medical bracelet around my wrist and ordered ER staff to transport me to the *east-wing.*

Having never been hospitalized, I was scared straight. Being hooked up to monitoring machines within minutes of being wheeled inside my room was so frightening, I deeply regretted going to the emergency room. And, before I could adapt to the surreal environment, the nurse began tapping veins on my right hand and forearm saying, *"You have perfectly soft and bouncy ones!"* as if referring to the curls in my hair. Looking at her as if she were insane, she then applied a tourniquet to distend the vein and inserted a ginormous needle into my forearm to start the blood IV, as I sat crying like a lost child.

Watching as the plastic pouch containing someone else's blood trickled inside my body was even more petrifying. Though told I needed to undergo several blood transfusions since I was practically bloodless when I arrived at the emergency room, I couldn't help thinking, *"Is this the blood of an evil-spirited murderer? And, will I adopt the same trait by having his or her blood inside my body?"* Fearing the worst, especially when later told I'd be infused with blood for ten days or more, I tried convincing myself it was the blood of Jesus—hoping to blot out the many negative thoughts that kept racing through my head.

Waking up the next morning, alone, was devastating considering my family was out of state and I hadn't notified anyone other than my neighbor. I remember thinking, *"If I were to die from fibroids while hospitalized, will my family at least receive a condolence call? Will I be carted off to a hospice to live out the rest of my days?"* While every thought imaginable swam through my mind, I assumed I was being, temporarily, hospitalized because my fibroids had become so large that they were affecting other parts of my body. I also assumed I'd be transfused back to health and discharged within a day or two.

However, the assigned doctor who visited me, later that morning, had something else in mind. After introducing herself, she mentioned that she had reviewed my medical history, blood test results, ultrasound reports, and had also spoken with my primary care doctor. She, then, informed me that I needed an *emergency hysterectomy*. Although I knew a lot about the procedure through research and while seeking medical opinions months' prior, just hearing her say the term triggered deep prayer that fibroids would miraculously grow legs and stampede out of me, to avoid surgery.

Nervously asking if I could be released once my blood stores were built back up so I could think about such highly invasive surgery, she gazed at me with empathy. Surely, in the back of my mind, I was plotting to *take the blood and run* in the same way I hauled tail out of a doctor's office after receiving a GnRHa injection to temporarily shrink fibroids.

When told being released wasn't an option because of my extremely low blood counts and grave anemic state, I expressed that I preferred myomectomy over having my uterus carved out and was willing to have as many of subsequent procedures as necessary to remove the droves of fibroids inside me. However, in a concerned manner, she told me that I could die on the operating table from massive blood loss if I were to undergo myomectomy—just as other doctors had said. I, then, proposed uterine fibroid embolization which she also nixed, explaining that the UFE procedure isn't recommended for women with large fibroids.

Since I wasn't a candidate for any other type of fibroid removal procedure, she insisted hysterectomy was my best bet and a permanent solution for my large, symptomatic fibroids. She, then, explained the various types of hysterectomy beginning with *supracervical hysterectomy*, the kind she recommended. Also referred to as *subtotal hysterectomy* or *partial hysterectomy*, the procedure involves removal of the upper portion of the uterus while leaving the cervix intact.[133]

Total hysterectomy also referred to as *traditional hysterectomy* or *complete hysterectomy* entails removal of the entire uterus and cervix.[134] *Total hysterectomy with salpingo-oophorectomy* involves removal of both ovaries and fallopian tubes as well as the uterus and cervix, especially when ovarian cancer or suspicious ovarian tumors are present.[135] And, *radical hysterectomy*, the most invasive type of hysterectomy that's performed when certain cancers are present and entails removal of the uterus, cervix, fallopian tubes, ovaries, pelvic lymph nodes, and upper portion of vagina.[136]

---

[133] "Hysterectomy." 1 Apr. 2017. *WebMD.com*, www.webmd.com/women/guide/hysterectomy#1.
[134] "Hysterectomy." 1 Apr. 2017. *WebMD.com*, www.webmd.com/women/guide/hysterectomy#1.
[135] "Hysterectomy." American College of Obstetricians and Gynecologists, Oct. 2018, www.acog.org/Patients/FAQs/Hysterectomy?IsMobileSet=false.
[136] "Hysterectomy." American College of Obstetricians and Gynecologists, Oct. 2018, www.acog.org/Patients/FAQs/Hysterectomy?IsMobileSet=false.

Suggesting partial abdominal hysterectomy not only made my stomach turn, I was zapped into early bereavement by the thought of being uterus-less. As she proceeded to educate me on the advantages of the procedure such as preserved sexual function and decreased risk of vaginal vault prolapse, she expounded on potential complications including extensive bleeding, infection, and accidental injury to other organs. Further mentioning that surgery would cause permanent scarring due to the likelihood of being cut both vertically and horizontally to remove my cantaloupe-size uterus, I began nervously rambling as if I had been thrown inside a lion's den.

I must have asked her a million questions including, *"Can I die from abdominal hysterectomy? How long is the recovery process? What medications will I need to take after surgery? Will this type of surgery affect my sex drive? How many abdominal hysterectomies have you performed? What are the complication rates? And, what if I refuse to undergo surgery?"*

While I'm sure she had several other lives to save that day, she answered them all caringly and professionally. However, as soon as she left my bedside, giving me a day to think it over, I became as *hysterical* as the surgical procedure term. To prevent falling apart, completely, I lay prostrate and prayed.

With less than twenty-four hours to decide whether to have the most invasive of fibroid procedures, I was so anxiety-riddled I could neither eat nor sleep. Learning through prior research that hysterectomy can cause memory loss, mood swings, and weight gain, terrified me.[137] Having read that sexual desire can be negatively impacted once the uterus is removed[138], petrified me. And, knowing I could never give birth, biologically, mortified me to tears.

As my mind kept racing, I tried focusing on the pros of hysterectomy. Being a surefire way of ridding my body of fibroids, permanently, meant I would no longer haul around a uterus the size of a six-month pregnancy, I thought. I would also avoid suffering another decade or so waiting for the onset of menopause that would, hopefully, shrink my fibroids.

Since my ovaries would be spared, I could have them

---

[137] "Adverse Effects Data." Hysterectomy Educational Resources and Service Foundation (HERS Foundation), 2018, www.hersfoundation.org/adverse-effects-data/.
[138] "Adverse Effects Data." Hysterectomy Educational Resources and Service Foundation (HERS Foundation), 2018, www.hersfoundation.org/adverse-effects-data/.

harvested and implanted into a surrogate in the event I wanted children down the line. And, knowing there was nothing more my health care providers could do for my humongous fibroids and horrifying symptoms, other than watch and wait for them to grow even larger, emergency hysterectomy seemed like the right choice. It was my only choice.

The following morning, the doctor accompanied by a nurse visited to discuss my decision. I assumed the nurse was present to review the consent forms with me as well as be a witness to my signing my uterus away. As I cried during the bittersweet moment, I kept reassuring myself, *"I want my life back. I want to feel normal again. And, I want to do all the things I loved doing before fibroids ransacked my life."*

Thereafter, the doctor informed me that both she and another surgeon would perform the partial abdominal hysterectomy. She also mentioned the location in which the surgery would take place and type of anesthesia I'd likely receive. I was, then, given a battery of tests including another pelvic exam, Pap Smear, endometrial biopsy, basic metabolic panel, kidney function test, electrocardiogram, blood glucose test, pulmonary function test, blood clotting test, and even a pregnancy test.

Experiencing a multitude of physical and emotional roller coaster rides while hospitalized, it's surprising I didn't go AWOL. Absent without official leave, that is. Numerous gurney and wheelchair excursions from exam room to exam room, for tests after tests, made me feel as if I were being wheeled around the country. And, with medical staff constantly entering my room to check my vitals and swap empty blood bags and medicine packs, surely, I often thought about snatching a needle off the nurse's tray and bursting the heck out of them all.

As frequently as blood was infused phlebotomists, like thieves in the night, would draw it right back out. Appearing wee hours of the morning to extract blood from my swollen veins was so painful and insomnia-inducing, I'd either ask, *"Since my veins are inflamed and I'm tired, is it possible to do this later? Perhaps, after breakfast or lunch?"* or *"Wouldn't it be easier and less taxing on my veins if I were given a bucket or two of blood, by mouth?"*

While my somewhat sarcastic questions and remarks usually made them chuckle, I was dead serious. Yet, they proceeded to suck the living blood out of me, insisting it had to be drawn, every morning, to ensure blood type match and test for viruses and infectious diseases. Though painful and inconvenient, I knew the ongoing blood infusing and drawing process was necessary to increase my hemoglobin, hematocrit, red blood cells, platelets and iron counts before my fibroid-infested uterus could be removed.

In fact, when admitted to the hospital and given another complete blood count test, my levels were even lower. Evidently, I was a member of the walking dead society and at risk of having a stroke. And, surprisingly, I didn't when my elderly roommate went into cardiac arrest on the third day of my hospital stay.

As doctors, nurses, and staff came rushing in with all kinds of medical equipment yelling, *"Code blue, code blue!"* while speaking in incomprehensible medical language, I was tempted to run out and hide in someone else's room. Hearing loud, guttural sighs as she turned every shade of blue, I presumed food had either gone down the wrong pipe; the meal was contaminated; or something along those lines.

Though hungrier than a hostage, I immediately stopped eating my lunch fearing my heart would suddenly stop beating too.

Hoping the recent round of blood transfusion would kill my hunger pains, I sat in bed highly on edge and famished. And, as soon as I saw a sheet placed over my roommate's body, after ten minutes or so, my appetite vanished.

Apparently, my *dead mate* had drifted off to either heaven or hell. And, I was shaken with such an elevated flight response, I'm surprised I didn't detach every needle, seemingly, lodged in each vein in my body, except my neck, and hightailed it out of the window. Viewing a body at a wake or funeral is one thing but seeing a corpse at a reach-out-and-touch distance was outright traumatizing.

As they wheeled her out of the room, I both prayed and envisioned her being taken to the hospitals' morgue. However, hours later, I heard through the *nursevine* that she was resuscitated and living with another roommate, hospital mate, or whatever they're called.

Giddyup Gurney…Go!

Overwhelmed by practically everything while hospitalized, I couldn't wait for the surgeons to carve, chop, slice, dice, or do whatever necessary to remove my monstrous fibroids. Anticipating how ecstatic I'd feel, no longer having to tolerate heavy bleeding, excruciating pain, and multitudes of other horrendous symptoms I endured for 15 years, I began counting down the days.

Scheduled in wee hours of the morning, I was given instructions outlining what to do the day before surgery. Since I couldn't drink or eat anything twelve hours prior, I requested a second helping of lunch thinking it could very well be my *last supper*—in the event I didn't make it out of surgery alive. At least, I'd transcend into heaven on a full stomach, I thought. However, all I had eaten came blasting out of me after taking an oral bowel cleansing solution, as required.

I was also instructed to shower that evening. Considering I hadn't due to the hospital's protocol that only allowed pre-surgery showers, I was long overdue. Just the thought of lying on the operating table, smelling as musky as mussels, made me even more enthusiastic about showering. Therefore, medical staff helped me out of bed, covered the IV sites with plastic, and moved me and the IV stand into the small bathroom.

Once inside, I spent several minutes trying to disrobe without ripping needles out of my veins; causing blood and medicine bags to hit the floor; or both. Unable to loosen the knots on my hospital gown, I cracked the door open and began shouting, *"Help! Can someone please help me!"* Within seconds, a nurse's aide came to my rescue and tried loosening them. As incapable as I, she exited the bathroom and returned minutes later with a fresh gown and a pair of medical scissors. While cutting me out of it and tossing it in the waste basket, she suggested I use the emergency pull string if I needed further assistance.

Taking what felt like a shower from hell with the IV stand inches away from my body and lukewarm water splashing everywhere, I soaped and rinsed in less than ten minutes. The idea of washing my hair went as fast as it came, as shampooing and rinsing would have taken forever. Therefore, I stepped out of the shower and began doing the tango with the IV stand, just so I could dry my body. Surprisingly, I didn't slip and break my neck.

Unable to put the hospital gown on while connected to tubes

dangling from the IV stand, I yanked the emergency pull string. A few minutes later, the same nurse's aide appeared, wrapped a towel around me, and escorted me to my bed. After drawing the curtain, she took the blood and medicine bags off the hooks and placed them in my right hand. She, then, guided the bags and tubing through the right sleeve. After rehanging the bags on the hooks, she placed my arm into the left sleeve and knotted only the upper back tie.

Although amazed by her technique in getting me into the gown, I didn't want to shower ever again while hospitalized. The process was much too awkward and seeing my backside exposed through the gaping slit in the back, made me lose all sense of dignity. While I should've asked for two gowns for better coverage, I let it go since surgery was only a few hours away.

Later that evening, it was impossible to sleep because a male, sex-craved lunatic took up residence in a room two or three doors away. Seemingly having every psychiatric disorder known to medicine, he shouted profanities at everyone who entered his room. As I listened to the most vulgar language I'd ever heard as medical staff, repeatedly, told him to calm down, I felt like I was in an insane asylum. Thankfully, he was given a tranquilizer or other sedative, as he became as quiet as a mouse after an hour of raising sand. I, then, prayed for a positive surgery outcome and fell asleep.

When the knock came at around two-thirty in the morning, three or four operating room personnel appeared at my bedside. Looking like the medical mafia dressed in dark uniforms, bouffant-style caps, masks and gloves, they slid me off the bed and onto a stretcher. Being whisked out of the room, down the elevator, past several sets of swinging doors, and into the pre-operative holding area was so surreal, I kept pinching myself.

Having never been in an operating room, I was scared to death as my limbs trembled. However, when met by my doctor, one of two surgeons scheduled to perform the partial abdominal hysterectomy, I was much more at ease.

As she and the operating room team gathered around and assured me that I was going to be okay, I belted out a "Thank You" song I made up off the top of my head. Not knowing if I was going to live or die on that operating table, I was compelled to do something memorable.

By the surprised look on their faces, it was apparent they

had never seen a patient as excited about surgery. Certainly, their smiles and applauses made me feel a tad more confident the surgeon-duo weren't going to slip up and *cut my lights out*. In other words, kill me! And, after singing my *song of songs* and signing consent forms, I was wheeled into the operating room.

As I lay on the stretcher gazing at huge bulbs above me, I was introduced to the anesthesiologist. In reviewing my medical history, he explained the purpose and type of anesthesia I was going to receive. He also informed me of possible risks such as waking up during surgery, organ damage, and even death—all of which made me want to hop off the operating table and head home. While I assumed it was just formality, I would have preferred having the conversation before signing my life away.

Then, in came the other surgeon who was scheduled to perform the surgery. I suppose two were necessary in hauling out my enormous, fibroid-compacted uterus. As the female surgeon introduced us as I was being connected to all types of monitors, I kept staring at him as he looked familiar. And, as soon as she mentioned his name, my eyes must've bulged as wide as the spotlights above me.

At that point, I felt like asking the anesthesiologist to hand me the breathing mask so I could gas myself into oblivion. Evidently, he was the same oncologist who scared the heck out of me during a consultation months' prior. Wanting to perform another pelvic exam to check the size and shape of my uterus, even though I had undergone two or more of the same exams within that month, I refused, ran out of his office, and never contacted him again.

Now, face to face and at his mercy, I prayed he wouldn't attempt paying me back by either dismissing the anesthesiologist and snatching my uterus out with his bare hands or leaving sharp surgical instruments inside me after stitching me up. While I should have apologized by saying, *"I'm so sorry Doc, so please find it in your heart not to kill me."*, instead, I prayed like I'd never prayed before as the anesthesiologist placed the mask over my face. And, within seconds, I was knocked out.

Surgery lasted approximately four hours and I remained asleep until late afternoon. When I awoke, pain from having my skin, muscles, and abdominal wall slit open to remove my gargantuan uterus was unimaginable. By far, it felt more brutal than passing truckloads of blood clots during my periods.

Unable to move a single bone in my body without feeling punishing pain, I begged the nurse to give me something more potent than the morphine drip that was trickling in my vein. Before doing so, she had to first determine the level of agony I was in. Therefore, she handed me a pain measurement chart and, indisputably, I pointed to the last icon which stood for *worst pain imaginable*.

Leaving my bedside and returning with two pills and a cup of water an hour later, I wanted to wrap the IV lines around her neck and strangulate her for making me wait so long. On the other hand, I wanted to hug her for giving me more powerful drugs to help ease the violent, constant spasms. When I asked what type of pills they were, she said, *"hydromorphone."* Being a derivative of morphine, surely, I thought I'd end up a prescription drug junkie while recovering in the hospital.

Before heading back to *la la land*, I used my feet to shuffle the blankets below my hip. In seeing my stomach tightly wrapped in a large bandage, I began wailing. Rapt with joy and disbelief that fibroids were eradicated overnight after lugging them around in my uterus for fifteen years, I couldn't take my eyes off it. Emotionally stirred since it was, now, flatter than a pancake even with the thick bandage on it, I couldn't stop tears from flowing. Had I been able to move, I would've jumped out of bed and put on a happy dance.

Though saddened that I didn't have any visitors to rejoice with me in my *"I'm no longer six-months pregnant with fibroids!"* moment, I was so heavily medicated I probably wouldn't have recognized them. While my parents had planned to fly to California, I told them to wait until I recovered as I didn't want them to see me all bandaged up and attached to tubes. Instead, they and my other family members continuously called before and after surgery. Therefore, the loneliness wasn't too bad.

Thankfully, my fantastic neighbor who was the last familiar face I saw before I collapsed, came to visit me a day or two after I was admitted. Clueless as to why I was in the hospital, I briefly shared with him that I had extremely large fibroids and needed to have an operation to remove them. Also concerned about the welfare of my dog, he asked that I give him the key to my apartment so he can feed and walk him.

As I continued looking at my stomach for what felt like twenty minutes, surprisingly, the stitches and staples didn't disengage when I caught glimpse of the urinary catheter that was stuck in my bladder. Staring at my urine in the plastic drainage bag that hung on the side on my bed, made me feel as if I had aged fifty years between undergoing surgery and waking up. However, the nurse mentioned the *pee-pee pack* would likely be removed within twenty-four hours. So, I was *relieved* about that.

While fading in and out of sleep that evening, the female surgeon came to check up on me. Like an angel, she asked how I was feeling. As I thanked her to no end for being an excellent doctor and surgeon, I asked, *"What did those horrible fibroids look like and how big were they?"* Grimacing and shaking her head, she said something like, *"You had several large ones that weighed five pounds."*

Knowing a normal, adult uterus weighs approximately sixty grams[139], I tried visualizing just how large and heavy five pounds of fibroids could be. At first, I envisioned the weight of a five-pound chicken. Suddenly realizing the five pounds of fibroids removed

---

[139] Daftary, SN. and Chakravarti, S. "Holland And Brews Manual of Obstetrics." 3rd Ed., Chap. 1, p. 3. Elsevier Health Sciences, 2011.

were equivalent to the five-pound bag of red delicious apples I bought days before landing in the emergency room, I'm surprised I didn't faint.

Confirming both vertical and horizontal incisions were necessary to remove my large uterus, she mentioned that she could only imagine how miserable I must have been living with that many fibroids and inherent symptoms as long as I had. She also informed me that I'd remain hospitalized for an undetermined number of days, as I needed more rounds of blood transfusions to replace all that was lost during surgery.

The next morning, I awoke hungrier than a wildebeest and thirstier than a fish out of water. Since I neither ate nor drank anything for the past twenty-four hours or so, I requested the breakfast menu. When told that I could only have water until evening because the surgeons had to ensure my intestines and bladder were functioning properly, surely, I wished I had the strength to leap out of bed and raid the hospital's food supply.

When evening came, I awaited the beef stew concoction that I, usually, chose from the dinner menu. However, I was given a pitcher of water, apple juice, and crackers which I gulfed down in seconds. A few minutes later, I buzzed the main desk to inform them that I needed to excrete. And, instead of being escorted to the bathroom, a portable toilet was wheeled into the room, instead.

As two medical staff slowly lifted me off the bed, raised my hospital gown above my waist, and lowered me onto the toilet, my pride instantly nosedived. Even though I wished I had owned one when I had hellish periods, sitting on a portable toilet surrounded by others was beyond embarrassing.

Unable to defecate and frustrated that I needed assistance in doing so, I was placed back in bed and given two more pitchers of water to drink. Minutes later, diarrhea struck and medical staff helped move me to the portable toilet, once again. Although I felt relieved after having my first post-surgery, bowel movement, my poor roommate must've passed out from the bellowing scent that permeated the thin curtain that separated us. Certainly, it would've been less humiliating had staffers sprayed the room with air freshener, I thought. Strapping on adult diapers, for which I was accustomed, may have also prevented the room from reeking.

The following day, a physical therapist appeared at my bedside, after lunch, and informed me that I needed to walk. Still in cruel pain and feeling lethargic, I assumed she had entered the wrong room. And, when I asked, *"Are you sure you have the right patient because I just came out of major surgery, two days ago, and pain is so overwhelming I can't even use the bathroom on my own?"*, she looked at my wristband and said, *"Yes, I'm here to help you walk to prevent blood clots from forming in your legs."*

While I hadn't heard of blood clots of the leg before, just hearing her say those two words immediately triggered thoughts of my horrific, heavy bleeding periods. Further explaining that a single clot can travel through the bloodstream and into the lungs, leading to complications like pulmonary embolism and even death made me so frightened, I concurred.

She, then, instructed medical staff to help me to my feet. As I stood on what felt like ancient bones with my legs trembling uncontrollably; hands grasped firmly onto the walker handles; and derriere jutting out of my gown, surely, I reconsidered living past the age of sixty-five.

As I shuffled out of the room hunched over and feeling like I'd been socked in the stomach in rapid succession, tears of pain began pouring. Empathetically, the physical therapist insisted that

I take my time while trying to convince me of the benefits of walking up and down the corridor to ease post-surgery pain.

In following her advice, I took baby steps until I reached the second or third patient room. Unable to go any further, she assisted in turning my body around and we headed back. Upon returning to my room, I was so wiped out that I slept through dinner.

The next day, at roughly the same time, the physical therapist engaged me in another *workout*. Seemingly, hell bent on torturing me knowing pain was unbearable, I walked alongside her anyway. Managing to walk past the main reception area and back to my room, while applying movement and breathing exercises she had taught me, was definitely an improvement in comparison to the previous day. And, from that day forward, she determined I could walk on my own and recommended I ask medical staff to assist me out of bed two or three times a day.

During the remaining days of post-surgery recovery, thankfully, nothing too untoward occurred. Other than receiving continuous intravenous blood and morphine infusions; breathing through a plastic device called an *incentive spirometer* to keep my lungs clear; having my vitals monitored regularly; taking walks up and down the hospital's corridor; hoping I'd be served food that looked and tasted familiar; and constantly asking medical staff when I'd be released, each day was as routine as it gets.

When, finally, discharged on February 18, 2009, I was given a bundle of documents to sign; discharge instructions; multivitamins to balance my hormones; a set of crutches, and oxycodone for pain. Having reservations about taking the opioid with scary street names such as *oxycotton*, *percs*, and *hillbilly heroin*, I expressed concern about the change in pain medication. Though the discharge nurse explained oxycodone is less addicting than morphine, I didn't feel any better about consuming them. But, since I had already felt like a full-blown junkie after undergoing surgery, I figured a few weeks of opioid use would neither kill me nor require addiction treatment.

Riding Down Recovery Road

Inhaling February's crisp air, after seventeen days in the hospital, was an out-of-body experience. However, seeing my car parked in the same spot, instantly, reminded me of all the dread prior to arriving at the emergency room. Bleeding for more than thirty consecutive days. The blood clots. The pain. The collapse.

Asking the male transportation aide to put the brakes on my wheelchair, I began silently praying. Had I been physically able to drop to my knees to express how grateful I was to be alive, knowing anything could have gone wrong during surgery, I would have. Yet, I sat praising God for giving me strength to bear all that I had gone through for 15 years; foresight in making the decision to undergo hysterectomy; confidence in knowing He would oversee the hands of both surgeons; and faith in pressing on as He would see me through it all.

Aware of my level of pain at discharge, the aide first laid the crutches on the back seat, then carefully lifted me onto my feet. Propping my right arm on top of the car, he bent down to raise my right leg and place it inside the car. Helping me pivot and lower my body onto the seat, with least pain, took several minutes. He, then, moved my left leg inside the car.

Instinctively grabbing hold of the seat belt as I normally would caused such severe shooting pain, I screamed aloud. Racing to the passenger side, he climbed in to secure it around my waist. Surely, every joint and muscle in his body must've ached, for days, after all he did in transferring me from wheelchair to car, that morning.

Driving home in pain, encased in a post-surgical abdominal binder and numbness in both legs, was more nerve-wracking than my first driving test. While I should've either hired a cab or planned to have someone pick me up, I feared my car would be towed. I also didn't want to inconvenience anyone since I was less than a mile away from home. Therefore, I pulled over to the curb twice for the safety of others and to wait for pain to lessen. Then, I slowly drove on side roads until I reached home.

Getting out of the car was far more challenging than getting in. Without any assistance, I knew it would take a while. Sliding my body to the edge of the seat while grabbing onto the wheel triggered spasms so disabling, I had to stop after the first attempt. Feeling defeated, I sat for ten minutes or so trying to come up with another strategy.

After taking a deep breath, I lifted and placed my left foot on the ground. Turning my body toward the door, I lifted my right leg and did the same. Simultaneously pressing my right hand on top of the dashboard while grasping the inner door frame with my left hand, with all my might, I finally stood to my feet.

Taking several minutes to adjust to blinding pain obviously triggered by my abrupt movements, I opened the back door and grabbed hold of the crutches. Hobbling with them saddled under my arms not only caused more pressure on my abdomen, they felt terribly awkward since I had never used crutches before.

As I shuffled to the doorstep at a snail's pace, I could hear my dog barking at the top of his lungs and clawing at the door. While dying to see him too, I had to figure out how to retrieve the key my neighbor had left under the doormat. Since it was virtually impossible to bend forward, I used the bottom of a crutch to flip the mat over and slide the key closer to my feet. Then, I held onto the doorknob and slowly lowered myself onto one knee—being more concerned about opening the incisions than lancinating pain I felt. Once I grasped the key, I hoisted myself back onto my feet, similarly.

As soon as I opened the door, my angel of a dog went completely berserk. Leaping up and down, while displaying the purest of love and every other emotion, made me burst into tears. With his high-pitched yelps nearly blasting my ears off, I tried my best to calm him. However, he remained uncontrollable as he spoke in dog language and likely said, *"I've missed you like crazy and thought I'd never see you again! Please don't ever leave me for such a long time again!"*

He must've gone bananas sitting at the door, day in and out, awaiting my return, I thought. He must've also felt a strong sense of abandonment. In fact, a few years before surgery, I rescued my smart and ultrasensitive dog. Likewise, he *rescued* me when I collapsed. Creating an everlasting bond, from that moment forward, I sensed he knew I was in pain. And, as I limped toward the couch, his overwhelming excitement subsided and he began licking my sandaled feet in attempt to make me feel better.

While recovery from partial abdominal hysterectomy is said to take approximately six to eight weeks, it took four months to completely heal. I suppose being sliced both vertically (from my navel to just above my pubic bone), and horizontally (roughly an inch above my pubic bone), to remove my humongous uterus was likely the reason why it took longer.

During the first two weeks, pain was so agonizing I couldn't do anything without shrieking—even while on painkillers. Sitting on furniture was most unbearable as I had to stand close to the edge of the chair or couch, hold onto the arms, then lower my body onto it, praying I wouldn't keel over. Rising from either chair or couch would also make me scream as I slid to the edge and used a crutch to stand. Had there been such a thing as adult high chairs, surely, I would've purchased one to prevent exacerbated pain whenever I sat or stood.

Getting in bed was just as painful and difficult. Although the hospital's physical therapist offered tips, prior to discharge, nothing seemed to work. To prevent placing pressure on my abdomen, I'd brace my hands on the nightstand to raise myself onto the bed. However, lifting my legs onto the bed was near impossible considering I could neither lean forward nor backward without experiencing brutal pain.

Maneuvering out of bed was also devastatingly painful.

Slowly swaying from side to side with my legs extended, I'd use my derriere and elbows to scoot to the bottom edge of the bed so I could clutch onto the bedpost and sit upright. Once my feet were on the floor, I usually had to wait for burning pain to ease before standing. But, over time, I learned to position my body closer to the headboard, so my legs could easily dangle off the bed without causing as much pain.

Bouts of gas and constipation may have intensified pain as well as contributed to my inability to sleep more than three or four hours, at a time. Therefore, I took laxatives and drank plenty of water as recommended in the recovery care material I was given. And, by the third week, I was able to sleep for longer periods as both symptoms disappeared.

I also experienced reddish-brownish vaginal bleeding which not only frightened me, it brought back memories of suffering with fibroids. Never wanting to see another sanitary pad ever again, I wore panty liners since the discharge was relatively light. I suppose wearing them for the very first time was somewhat joyous, knowing I couldn't fathom wearing panty liners in the past.

Required to see the female doctor who performed the

surgery, once a week and for approximately a month, I shared the discharge issue with her during the first visit. Mentioning that vaginal drainage after hysterectomy was normal and would gradually taper off in a few days, put me at ease.

Thereafter, she removed the bandages and I nearly died when I saw the stapled incisions for the first time. As if it had been gutted like a fish, redness and swelling looked utterly horrifying. And, my belly button looked as if it had been snipped off during surgery. After assuring me it would eventually return to normal, she changed bandages, assessed my pain level, and scheduled a follow-up appointment to remove the staples.

Having noticeable scars from vertical and horizontal incisions took some time getting used to since I didn't have any on my body, prior to surgery. Feeling deformed every time I'd steal glances while cleaning them and knowing I could no longer wear a bikini was a tough pill to swallow. Consumed with figuring out what I'd say when asked why I had such large scars on my abdomen and pelvis, especially by a future significant other, was also taxing.

Additionally, having read that some women experience a decrease in sex drive after abdominal hysterectomy, made me dreadfully afraid my *absentee uterus* would cause my sexual desire to vanish. But, thankfully, my libido wasn't compromised. And, once I fully recovered, my sexual appetite was alive, well, and functioning better than ever before.

The most petrifying aspect of hysterectomy, that hit like a ton of bricks, was coming to terms with never being able to have biological children. Throughout recovery and several years thereafter, the mere thought of my baby-making days being over would often trigger tears. Though overwhelmed with sadness, I'd force myself to look on the bright side knowing I was, now, free of fibroids and able to enjoy life again. I'd also remind myself that surrogacy was a possibility since my ovaries were left intact.

With respect to some women who believe hysterectomy is unnatural, unethical, and should never be an alternative, suffering with symptomatic, uterine fibroid tumors that caused a barrage of havoc-wreaking symptoms made me view the surgical procedure through a lens that only I could. Tolerating such uncontrollable symptoms until menopause, with hopes *change of life* would diminish them, wasn't a chance I was going to take. "*What if menopause starts in my late 50s and fibroids fail to shrink?*", I often thought.

Since I wasn't a candidate for any other fibroid procedure because my enlarged uterus was filled with *five pounds of fibroids* and was getting nowhere fast with blind optimism, questionable medical advice, pharmaceutical quick fixes, and fear, hysterectomy was the only way to restore my quality of life, at age 43. By no means, did I feel less womanly because my uterus was removed. Instead, hysterectomy has made me feel like I am *more woman* as I no longer have to spend extended periods on the toilet watching clumps of blood clots and endometrial casts drop out of me; tolerate cramping pain; pop pain pills; ruin my furniture and that of others; feel isolated; dodge social activities; call out sick from work; purchase heaps of sanitary products; and plan my life around my horrific periods and rapidly growing fibroids.

After riding down recovery road and fully regaining physical strength, I resumed many of my favorite activities. Passionate about ice-skating since adolescence, I was thrilled to hit the rink again. Gliding across the ice, dressed in a leotard, short ruffled skirt, and leggings was so blissfully revitalizing, I felt like a gold medalist as I performed the same jumps and moves I did as a teenager.

Equally passionate about roller-skating, I feverishly searched for local rinks. Unable to find any within the surrounding area in which I lived, I traveled over fifteen miles just to enjoy a recreational activity I've always loved. Later discovering a rink much closer, I frequented it practically every weekend. From opening until closing, I'd dance on wheels, skate backwards, and speed skate too.

Across the board, hysterectomy has made a dramatic difference in my life. Most thrilling is being able to wear white, a color I could only dream of wearing from the waist down. In fact, I went on a shopping spree in celebration of being freed from the bondage of fibroids, shortly after recovery. As I gazed in the window of my favorite department store and saw the most beautiful, white dress on a mannequin, I had to catch my breath. Thinking out loud, *"Wow, I can actually wear that dress any day of the month and without any fear of bloodstains!"*, not only made my eyes well up, I ended up purchasing two of them. I also bought a skirt and a pair of jeans—both of which were as white as snow.

Like a computer, had life come bundled with a restart button,

I would have resolutely pressed it to start life all over again. Undoubtedly, the outcome would have been much different had I known, then, what I know now. While there isn't a perfect roadmap in figuring out what to do and where to start when fibroids begin disrupting your life, experience has taught me that the first step is to demand ultrasound or other type of imaging test.

The manual uterine palpation exam or *touch test*, followed by all too common remarks some women with fibroids hear including *'Fibroids are normal and many women have them'*, *'Fibroids generally grow during menstruation and usually return to normal sizes after menstruation'*, *'Since they feel relatively small and are asymptomatic, there's no need to worry'*, *'Birth control pills and pain medication should keep fibroids at bay'* and *'Since they aren't causing any symptoms, let's watch and wait until they do'*, is not a diagnosis of fibroids and can be misleading.

Upon receiving copies of the results and images, requesting that health care providers furnish layperson explanations of the findings is vital. Since some aren't patient-centric and others don't have the gift of time to provide in depth information regarding ultrasound results, fibroids, and treatment options, seeking those who are caring, compassionate, and willing to share such important information with patients is crucial.

Proactively conducting research to learn about the disorder including types, characteristics, and location of fibroids within the uterus; common symptoms; types of available procedures; and pros, cons, and potential risks of each procedure is not only beneficial, self-acquired knowledge encourages improved participation and discussions with health care providers on treatment options based on the size of fibroids, symptoms, overall health, and desire to have children.

Furthermore, asking for referrals to specialists and seeking multiple opinions is important. Speaking with women who've struggled with symptomatic, uterine fibroid tumors and have undergone procedures to shrink, remove, or permanently remove them, is equally imperative—as women who've *been there* will likely offer invaluable information that only comes with experience.

Evidently, every woman's body and case of fibroids is unique. However, there is commonality of truth. And, considering the truth sets one free, it's important to be honest when informing health care providers about symptoms and coping mechanisms.

Downplaying either due to shame, embarrassment, and fear can delay intervention, diminish candidacy for certain procedures, and pave the way for continual growth spurts. By building a trusting partnership, treatment can be mutually and timely decided upon and quality of life is restored—which every woman with symptomatic, uterine fibroid tumors deserves.

After full recovery, I remember walking my adorable, life-saving dog, Prince, at around eleven o'clock one evening. Hearing birds sing for the first time in 15 years was on par with spiritual rebirth. Being completely shut out of life while battling symptomatic, uterine fibroid tumors, I had no idea they came out at night.

Looking up and watching them pounce about the branches, I felt as if the birds were talking to me in their sing-song language. By faith, they were letting me know I was now free. Free of fibroids. Free to soar. Free to be me. And, free to *openly* share my journey.

An Open Letter

Dear Shelley Susman, M.D. and Scott Eisenkop, M.D.:

An open acknowledgment is the least return I can render to both of you for saving my life.

With a long-standing case of symptomatic, uterine fibroid tumors, I assumed I would either bleed to death or have a heart attack—especially due to my critically low hemoglobin and platelets counts. If it hadn't been for your extraordinary expertise, disposition, and advice, surely, one of the above may have occurred.

Therefore, I am compelled to assert that you are great assets to the medical profession and the epitome of every patient's wish in having experienced, empathetic, approachable, and respectful surgeons on their side. You went above and beyond, consistently displaying each of these fine qualities, before, during, and after surgery.

From the moment I landed in the emergency room and throughout my seventeen-day hospital stay, your expression of undying care, concern, and compassion was unparalleled. You minimized my fears, tears, anxiety, and multitude of other nerve-wracking emotions which made my journey endurable.

While words may appear inadequate in expressing my heartfelt gratitude and appreciation, I sincerely thank you for performing a successful, partial abdominal hysterectomy on me in February of 2009. After removal of *five pounds of fibroids*, I headed down recovery road victoriously and my health and well-being has been fully restored.

Surgeons like you are rare and I am fortunate that my life was placed in your expert hands. Like towers of strength, both of you, your operating room team, and medical staff at Sherman Oaks Hospital extended my life. For this, may you all be blessed, forever.

With great gratitude and appreciation,

Rose Marie Johnson
Author, Sufferer, Survivor and Research Advocate
five pounds of fibroids: a memoir

Medical Reports / Test Results

Patient name : JOHNSON, ROSE
File number : 46532-05
Date of exam : 1/31/05
Physician :

1st ultrasound ordered at age 39 (2005)

PELVIC ULTRASOUND:

Clinical history: uterine fibroid. Heavy menstrual bleeding.

Several images in transverse and sagittal directions through the abdomen were obtained.

The uterus is markedly enlarged and measures 16 cm in length and 9.5 cm anteroposterior and 11.3 cm wide. There is markedly inhomogeneous parenchymal pattern with multiple hypoechoic uterine masses and demonstrates nodular uterine margin. There is central hyper echoic density 9.5 mm in thickness, which probably represents endometrial echo possible premenstrual proliferation. Ovarian echoes demonstrate no adnexal masses. No free cul de sac fluid can be detected.

IMPRESSION:

1- Multiple enlarged uterine fibroid.

THANK YOU FOR THE OPPORTUNITY TO ASSIST WITH YOUR PATIENT.

PATIENT NAME: JOHNSON, ROSE MRN : N211334
AGE: 42

2nd ultrasound ordered at age 42 (2008)

EXAM DATE: 05/01/08 ACCESSION :
MODALITY : US
EXAMINATION: PELVIS COMPLETE

IMPRESSION:

1. The uterus is extremely enlarged, with heterogeneous echogenicity, most likely representing a very large leiomyomatous uterus. The ovaries could be visualized because of the enlarged size of the uterus. Clinical correlation and further evaluation with MRI is recommended, if clinically indicated.

INDICATION FOR SCAN:

History of fibroids. Heavy bleeding.

FINDINGS:

The uterus is very enlarged, with heterogeneous echogenicity. It measures 24 x 10 x 12 cm in size. Because of its enlarged size, the ovaries cannot be visualized. This is most consistent with a large leiomyomatous uterus. Clinical correlation is recommended and further evaluation with MRI, if clinically indicated. No definite adnexal masses are seen. There is no evidence of free fluid in the cul-de-sac.

Thank you for referring this patient.

Complete Blood Count (CBC) ordered at age 42 (2008) Note: Age indicated below is in error

PATIENT NAME: Johnson, Rosemarie | AGE: 43 | SEX: F
PAGE: 2 | COLLECTION DATE: 4/25/2008 | LOG-IN DATE: 4/25/2008 | REPORT DATE: 4/29/2008

REMARKS
Draw Date & Time: 4/25/2008

REPORT STATUS: FINAL

TEST	RESULT IN RANGE	RESULT OUT OF RANGE	UNITS	REFERENCE RANGE
IRON		8 L	ug/dL	45-180
Result verified by repeat analysis.				
TIBC (Calc.)	424		ug/dL	200-460
% SATURATION		2 L	%	15-50
SPECIAL CHEMISTRY				
GLYCOHGB (A1C)		3.8 L	%	4.0-6.2
TUMOR MARKERS				
CA-125 (OM-MA)	4		U/mL	<21

Methodology: DPC IMMULITE 2000
Results greater than or equal to 21 U/mL may be found in a small percentage of healthy individuals and in patients with non-malignant conditions, such as pericarditis, cirrhosis, severe hepatic necrosis, endometriosis, first trimester pregnancy, and ovarian cysts, or inpatients with non-ovarian malignancies, such as uterine carcinoma, hepatoma, pancreatic adenocarcinoma, and lung cancers.
A result below 21 U/mL does not necessarily inidcate the absence of residual or recurrent ovarian cancer because some patients with histopathological evidence of ovarian carcinoma may have CA-125 measurement below 21 U/mL.

TEST	RESULT IN RANGE	RESULT OUT OF RANGE	UNITS	REFERENCE RANGE
HEMATOLOGY				
WBC	7.20		10*3/ul	4.0-11.0
RBC		3.34 L	10*6/ul	3.9-5.1
HGB		5.7 CL	g/dL	11.0-16.0
Hemogram verified by repeat analysis.				
HCT		19.9 L	%	35-47
MCV		59.5 L	fL	80.0-100.0
MCH		17.1 L	pg	27.0-34.0
MCHC		28.7 L	g/dL	31.0-36.0
RDW		23.0 H	%	10.0-15.2
MPV	6.4		fL	5.2-11.1
PLATELETS		39 CL	10*3/ul	150-400
Hemogram verified by repeat analysis.				
AUTO-DIFFERENTIAL				
NEUTROPHILS %	64.9		%	45.0-70.0
LYMPHOCYTES %	22.4		%	15.0-50.0
MONOCYTES %	10.9		%	0.0-15.0
EOSINOPHILS %	1.1		%	0.0-5.0

Page 2: CONTINUED ON NEXT PAGE

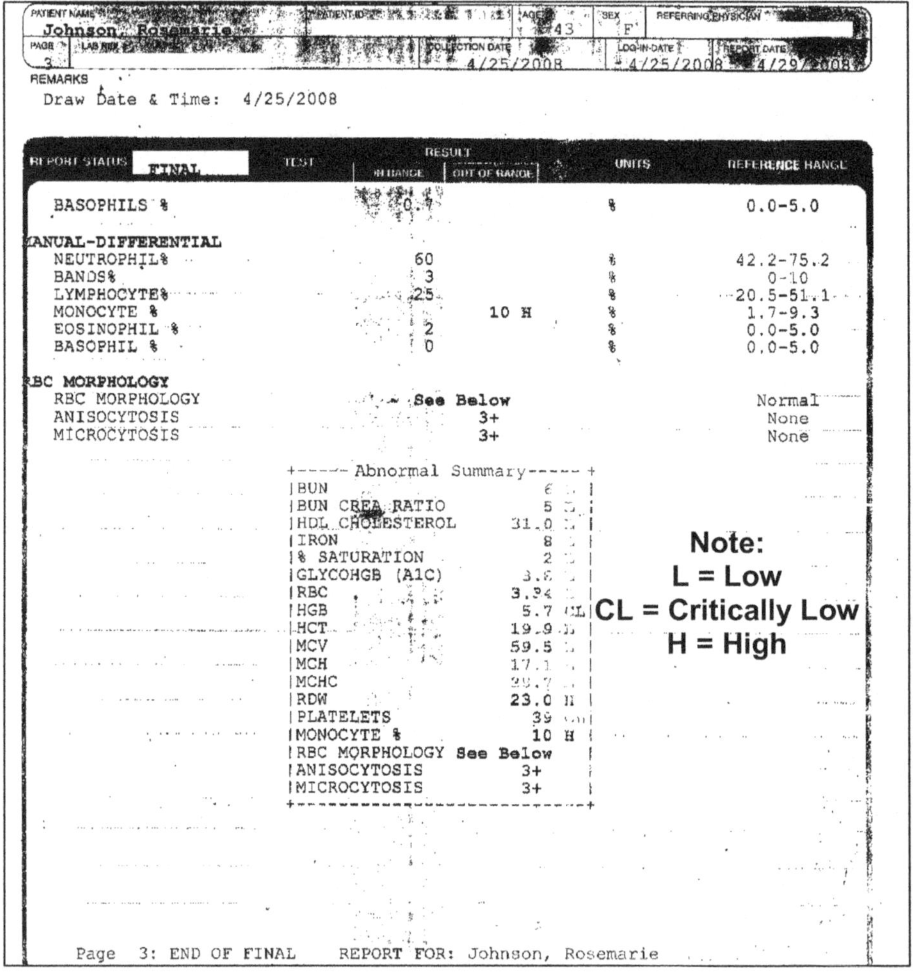

PATIENT NAME	AGE	SEX
Johnson, Rosemarie	43	F

PAGE	COLLECTION DATE	LOG-IN-DATE	REPORT DATE
3	4/25/2008	4/25/2008	4/29/2008

REMARKS
Draw Date & Time: 4/25/2008

REPORT STATUS **FINAL**

TEST	RESULT IN RANGE	RESULT OUT OF RANGE	UNITS	REFERENCE RANGE
BASOPHILS %	0.7		%	0.0-5.0
MANUAL-DIFFERENTIAL				
NEUTROPHIL%	60		%	42.2-75.2
BANDS%	3		%	0-10
LYMPHOCYTE%	25		%	20.5-51.1
MONOCYTE %		10 H	%	1.7-9.3
EOSINOPHIL %	2		%	0.0-5.0
BASOPHIL %	0		%	0.0-5.0
RBC MORPHOLOGY				
RBC MORPHOLOGY		**See Below**		Normal
ANISOCYTOSIS		3+		None
MICROCYTOSIS		3+		None

Abnormal Summary

Test	Result	Flag
BUN	6	[illegible]
BUN CREA RATIO	5	[illegible]
HDL CHOLESTEROL	31.0	[illegible]
IRON	8	[illegible]
% SATURATION	2	[illegible]
GLYCOHGB (A1C)	3.8	[illegible]
RBC	3.94	[illegible]
HGB	5.7	CL
HCT	19.9	[illegible]
MCV	59.5	[illegible]
MCH	17.1	[illegible]
MCHC	29.7	[illegible]
RDW	23.0	H
PLATELETS	39	[illegible]
MONOCYTE %	10	H
RBC MORPHOLOGY	**See Below**	
ANISOCYTOSIS	3+	
MICROCYTOSIS	3+	

Note:
L = Low
CL = Critically Low
H = High

Page 3: END OF FINAL REPORT FOR: Johnson, Rosemarie

Resources

Below is a list of resources on uterine fibroid tumors, treatment information, statistics, and forums. Please note that contact information may have changed since publication of this book.

American Association of Gynecologic Laparoscopists (AAGL)
6757 Katella Avenue
Cypress, CA 90630
(800) 554-2245
www.aagl.org

American College of Obstetricians and Gynecologists (ACOG)
409 12th St, SW
P.O. Box #96920
Washington, DC 20090
(800) 762-2264 Ext. #192
www.acog.org

Center for Disease Control and Prevention
1600 Clifton Road
Atlanta, GA 30329
(800) 232-4636
www.cdc.gov

Center for Uterine Fibroids (Brigham and Women's Hospital)
77 Avenue Louis Pasteur
New Research Building
Boston, MA 02115
(800) 722-5520
www.fibroids.net

Department of Health and Human Services (Food and Drug Administration)
5600 Fishers Lane
Rockville, MD 20857
(888) INFO-FDA
www.fda.gov

Hysterectomy Educational Resources and Services (HERS Foundation)
422 Bryn Mawr Avenue
Bala Cynwyd, PA 19004
(888) 750-HERS or (888) 750-4377
www.hersfoundation.org

HysterSisters
3091 College Park Drive
Suite #240-61
Conroe, TX 77384
(832) 663-7401
www.hystersisters.com

Medline Plus – U.S. National Library of Medicine
8600 Rockville Pike
Bethesda, MD 20894
(888) 346-3656
www.medlineplus.gov

National Institute of Environmental Health Sciences (NIEHS)
111 T.W. Alexander Drive
Research Triangle Park, NC 27709
(919) 541-3345
www.niehs.nih.gov

National Uterine Fibroids Foundation (NUFF)
P.O. Box 9688
Colorado Springs, CO 80932
(719) 633-3454
www.nuff.org

National Women's Health Network
P.O. Box #306
Portland, Maine 04112
(800) 798-7902
www.womenshealthnetwork.org

Office on Women's Health (OWH)
8270 Willow Oaks Corporate Drive
Fairfax, VA 22031
(800) 994-9662
www.womenshealth.gov

Resolve: The National Infertility Association
7918 Jones Branch Drive
Suite #300
McLean, VA 22102
(703) 556.7172
www.resolve.org

U.S. National Library of Medicine
8600 Rockville Pike
Bethesda, MD 20894
(888) 346-3656
www.nlm.nih.gov

The White Dress Project
1075 Peachtree Street NE
Suite #3650
Atlanta, GA 30309
(678) 796-TWDP
www.thewhitedressproject.com

Books

Below is a partial list of valuable books I read while searching for answers about uterine fibroid tumors and treatment options.

A Gynecologist's Second Opinion: The Questions and Answers You Need to Take Charge of Your Health
by William H. Parker, M.D.

Fibroid Tumors and Endometriosis
by Susan M. Lark, M.D.

Fibroids: The Complete Guide to Taking Charge of Your Physical, Emotional, and Sexual Well-Being
by Johanna Skilling

Healing Fibroids: A Doctor's Guide to a Natural Cure
by Allan Warshowsky, M.D. and Elena Oumano, PhD

It's a Sistah Thing: A Guide to Understanding and Dealing with Fibroids for Black Women
by Monique R. Brown

Natural Treatment of Fibroid Tumors and Endometriosis
by Susan M. Lark, M.D.

Our Bodies, Ourselves: A New Edition for a New Era
by Boston Women's Health Book Collective and Judy Norsigian

Sex, Lies, and the Truth About Uterine Fibroids: A Journey from Diagnosis to Treatment to Renewed Good Health
by Carla Dionne

The American Holistic Medical Association Guide to Holistic Health: Healing Therapies for Optimal Wellness
by Larry Trivieri, Jr.

The Complementary and Alternative Medicine Information Source Book
by Alan M. Rees

The Complete Book of Ayurvedic Home Remedies
by Vasant Lad, B.A.M.S, M.A.Sc.

The Fibroid Book: A Guide to Treating the Most Common Cause of Hysterectomy
by Francis L. Hutchins, Jr., M.D.

The First Year-Fibroids: An Essential Guide for the Newly Diagnosed
by Johanna Skilling

The No-Hysterectomy Option: Your Body-Your Choice
by Herbert A. Goldfarb, M.D. with Judith Greif, R.N.

The Official Patient's Sourcebook on Uterine Fibroids: A Revised and Updated Directory for the Internet Age
by James N. Parker, MD and Philip M. Parker, PhD

Treating Menstrual Cramps Naturally: Effective Natural Solutions for Discomforts Most Women Face
by Susan M. Lark, M.D.

Uterine Fibroids: The Complete Guide
by Elizabeth A. Stewart, M.D.

Uterine Fibroids: What Every Woman Needs to Know
by Nelson H. Stringer, M.D.

What Your Doctor May Not Tell You About Premenopause: Balance Your Hormones and Your Life from Thirty to Fifty by John R. Lee, Virginia Hopkins, and Jesse Hanley

Works Cited

"About Jin Shin Jyutsu." UC San Diego School of Medicine. Center for Integrative Medicine, 2018, www.medschool.ucsd.edu/som/fmph/research/cim/clinicalcare/Pages/jinshinjyutsu.aspx.

"Acupressure Points and Massage Treatment." WebMD Medical Reference, 21 Oct. 2017, Reviewed by Kiefer, D., WebMD, www.webmd.com/balance/guide/acupressure-points-and-massage-treatment#1.

"Adverse Effects Data." Hysterectomy Educational Resources and Service Foundation (HERS Foundation), 2018, www.hersfoundation.org/adverse-effects-data/.

"Anemia." American Society of Hematology. 2018. www.hematology.org/Patients/Anemia/.

"Anemia." Mayo Clinic. 8 Aug. 2017. www.mayoclinic.org/diseases-conditions/anemia/diagnosis-treatment/drc-20351366.

Baird, DD., Dunson, DB., et al. "High Cumulative Incidence of Uterine Leiomyoma in Black and White Women: Ultrasound Evidence." *AJOG,* Jan. 2003, Vol. 188, no. 1, pp. 100-107, doi.org/10.1067/mob.2003.99, Abstract.

Bellieni, CV., Pinto, I., et al. "Exposure to Electromagnetic Fields from Laptop Use of "Laptop" Computers." *Arch Environ Occup Health*, 2012, Vol. 67, no. 1, pp. 31-6, *PubMed*, www.ncbi.nlm.nih.gov/pubmed/22315933, Abstract.

The Bible. Authorized King James Version, Oxford University Press, 1998.

"Biotin." U.S. National Library of Medicine, 17 Sep. 2018. *MedlinePlus*, www.medlineplus.gov/druginfo/natural/313.html.

"Blue Cohosh." Natural Medicines Comprehensive Database Consumer Version. Therapeutic Research Faculty, 2018, *WebMD*, www.webmd.com/vitamins/ai/ingredientmono-987/blue-cohosh.

Bradley, L. "Menstrual Dysfunction." Aug. 2010. Cleveland Clinic. Center for Continuing Education. www.clevelandclinicmeded.com/medicalpubs/diseasemanagement/womens-health/menstrual-dysfunction/.

Carrie, written by Stephen King, directed by Brian De Palma, United Artists, 1976.

Complementary, Alternative, or Integrative Health: What's in a Name?" National Center for Complimentary and Integrative Health. 8 Nov. 2018, www./nccih.nih.gov/health/integrative-health.

Conner K. "The Sitz Bath in Gynecology." *Naturopathic Doctor News & Review*, 1 Feb. 2009, www.ndnr.com/womens-health/the-sitz-bath-in-gynecology.

Cornforth, T. "Benign Uterine Fibroid Tumors Types and Treatments." 19 May 2018. Reviewed by Shur, M., *VeryWellHealth*, www.verywellhealth.com/benign-uterine-fibroid-tumors-3520704.

Cozma-Petruţ, A., Loghin, F., et al. "Diet in Irritable Bowel Syndrome: What to Recommend, Not What to Forbid to Patients!" *World J Gastroenterol*, 2017, Vol. 23, no. 21, pp. 3771-3783, doi:10.3748/wjg.v23.i21.3771, Abstract.

"Cramp Bark." Natural Medicines Comprehensive Database Consumer Version. Therapeutic Research Faculty, 2018, *WebMD*, www.webmd.com/vitamins/ai/ingredientmono-746/cramp-bark.

Cunningham, J., Yonkers, KA., et al. "Update on Research and Treatment of Premenstrual Dysphoric Disorder." Apr. 2009, Vol. 17, no. 2, pp. 120-137. *Harv Rev Psychiatry*, doi:10.1080/10673220902891836, Abstract.

Daftary, SN. and Chakravarti, S. "Holland And Brews Manual of Obstetrics." 3rd Ed., Chap. 1, p. 3. Elsevier Health Sciences, 2011.

Dawood, MY. "Primary Dysmenorrhea: Advances in Pathogenesis and Management." *Obstet Gynecol*, Aug. 2006, Vol.108, no. 2, pp. 428-441, *National Center for Biotechnology Information*, www.ncbi.nlm.nih.gov/pubmed/16880317, Abstract.

"Diagnostic Laparoscopy." 24 May 2016. *MedlinePlu*s, www.medlineplus.gov/ency/article/003918.htm.

"Dietary Proteins." U.S. National Library of Medicine, 31 Jan. 2018. *MedlinePlus*, www.medlineplus.gov/dietaryproteins.html.

"Digital Rectal Exam (DRE)." Cedars-Sinai. 2018. www.cedars-sinai.edu/Patients/Programs-and-Services/Urology-Academic-Practice/Conditions-and-Treatments/Diagnostic-Testing/Digital-Rectal-Exam-DRE.aspx.

"Drospirenone and Ethinyl Estradiol (Oral Route)." 1 Oct. 2018. *Mayo Clinic*, www.mayoclinic.org/drugs-supplements/drospirenone-and-ethinyl-estradiol-oral-route/description/drg-20061917.

Dubey, N., Hoffman, JF., et al. "The ESC/E(Z) Complex, An Effector of Response to Ovarian Steroids, Manifests an Intrinsic Difference in Cells from Women with Premenstrual Dysphoric Disorder." *Molecular Psychiatry*, Aug. 2017, Vol. 22, pp. 1172-1184, doi:10.1038/mp.2016.229.

"Dysmenorrhea: Painful Periods." FAQ 046. *ACOG*, 2015, www.acog.org/Patients/FAQs/Dysmenorrhea-Painful-Periods.

"Endometriosis Symptoms, Diagnosis and Treatment." Brigham and Women's Hospital. 2018. www.brighamandwomens.org/obgyn/infertility-reproductive-surgery/endometriosis/endometriosis-guide-for-women.

"Evening Primrose Oil." National Center for Complementary and Integrative Health. Sep. 2016. *National Institutes of Health*, www.nccih.nih.gov/health/eveningprimrose.

"False Unicorn." Natural Medicines Comprehensive Database Consumer Version. Therapeutic Research Faculty, 2018, *WebMD*, www.webmd.com/vitamins/ai/ingredientmono-193/false-unicorn.

Fang, L., Xiao, X-F., et al. "Recent Advance in Studies on Angelica Sinensis." *Chin. Herb. Med*, 2012, Vol. 4, p. 12, doi:10.3969/j.issn.1674-6384.2012.01.004, Abstract.

"Fibroid FAQs." UCLA Obstetrics and Gynecology. 2018. UCLA Health, www.obgyn.ucla.edu/fibroid-faq.

"Fibroid-like Conditions: Adenomyosis and Endometrial Polyps." Brigham and Women's Hospital. 2018. www.brighamandwomens.org/obgyn/infertility-reproductive-surgery/cysts-and-fibroids/fibroid-line-conditions-adenomyosis-and-endometrial-polyps.

"Fibroids." UCLA Obstetrics and Gynecology. 2018. UCLA Health, www.obgyn.ucla.edu/fibroids.

"Fibroids: Symptoms, Treatment, Diagnosis." UCLA Obstetrics and Gynecology. 26 Mar. 2017. UCLA Health, www.obgyn.ucla.edu/fibroids.

"Fibroid Treatment Program." UCLA Obstetrics and Gynecology. 1 Apr. 2017. UCLA Health, www.obgyn.ucla.edu/fibroid-faq.

"Folic Acid." U.S. National Library of Medicine, 23 Oct. 2018. *MedlinePlus*, www.medlineplus.gov/folicacid.html.

"Genital HPV Infection - Fact Sheet: What is HPV?" 16 Nov. 2017. Centers for Disease Control and Prevention, www.cdc.gov/std/hpv/stdfact-hpv.htm.

Ghant, MS., Lawson AK., et al. "Beyond the Physical: A Qualitative Assessment of the Emotional Burden of Symptomatic Uterine Fibroids on Women's Mental Health." *Fertility and Sterility*, 21 Oct. 2014, Vol. 102, no. 3, ed. 248, doi.org/10.1016/j.fertnstert.2014.07.844, Abstract.

The Godfather, written by Mario Puzo, directed by Francis F. Coppola, performances by Brando, Marlon, Al Pacino, James Caan, Robert Duvall, Talia Shire, and Diane Keaton, Paramount Home Video, 1972.

Goodwin, SC. and Walker, WJ. "Uterine Artery Embolization for the Treatment of Uterine Fibroids." *Curr Opin Obstet Gynecol*, Sep. 1998, Vol. 10, no. 4, pp. 315-320, doi:10.1097/00001703-199808000-00006, Abstract.

Hackenberg, R., Gesenhues, T., et al. "The Response of Uterine Fibroids to GnRH-Agonist Treatment Can be Predicted in Most Cases After One Month." *Eur J Obstet Gynecol Reprod Biol*, 3 Jul. 1992, Vol. 45, no. 2, pp. 125-129, doi.org/10.1016/0028-2243(92)90228-Q, Abstract.

Halbreich, U. and Kahn LS. "Treatment of Premenstrual Dysphoric Disorder with Luteal Phase Dosing of Sertraline." *Expert Opin Pharmacother*, Nov. 2003, Vol. 4, no. 11, pp. 2065-2078, doi:10.1517/14656566.4.11.2065, Abstract.

Hertz, S. "The Benefits and Risks of Pain Relievers: Q & A on NSAIDs with Sharon Hertz, M.D." 26 Sep. 2018. Food and Drug Administration, www.fda.gov/ForConsumers/ConsumerUpdates/ucm107856.htm.

Hextall, A., Bidmead, J., et al. "The Impact of the Menstrual Cycle on Urinary Symptoms and the Results of Urodynamic Investigation." *BJOG*, Nov. 2001, Vol. 108, no. 11, pp. 1193-1196, doi.org/10.1111/j.1471-0528.2003.00280.x, Article.

Hörl, WH. "Nonsteroidal Anti-Inflammatory Drugs and the Kidney." Pharmaceuticals (Basel, Switzerland), Vol. 3, no. 7, pp. 2291-2321, 21 Jul. 2010, doi:10.3390/ph3072291, Abstract.

Huang, K-L. and Tsai, S-J. "St. John's Wort (Hypericum Perforatum) as a Treatment for Premenstrual Dysphoric Disorder: Case Report." *Int J Psychiatry Med*, 1 Sep. 2003, Vol. 33, no. 3, pp. 295-297, doi.org/10.2190/RERY-N6AC-NADC-EHY4, Abstract.

"Hysterectomy." 1 Apr. 2017. *WebMD.com*, www.webmd.com/women/guide/hysterectomy#1.

"Hysterectomy." American College of Obstetricians and Gynecologists, Oct. 2018, www.acog.org/Patients/FAQs/Hysterectomy?IsMobileSet=false

"Hysterosalpingogram." *Infertility and Reproduction Guide,* 1 Apr. 2017. *WebMD.com*, www.webmd.com/infertility-and-reproduction/guide/hysterosalpingogram-21590#1.

I Dream of Jeannie, written by Sidney Sheldon, directed by Gene Nelson, Hal Cooper, and Claudio Guzman, performances by Barbara Eden, Larry Hagman, Bill Daily, and Hayden Rorke, Sony Pictures Television, 1965.

Indman, PD. "Types of Uterine Fibroids." 19 Sep. 2011. *ObGYN.net*, www.obgyn.net/infertility/types-uterine-fibroids.

"Inositol." Natural Medicines Comprehensive Database Consumer Version. Therapeutic Research Faculty, 2018, *WebMD*, www.webmd.com/vitamins/ai/ingredientmono-299/inositol.

Invasion of the Body Snatchers, based on novel written by Jack Finney, directed by Phillip Kaufman, performances by Donald Sutherland, Brooke Adams, Leonard Nimoy, Jeff Goldblum and Veronica Cartwright, United Artists, 1978.

Johnson-Wimbley, TD. and Graham, DY. "Diagnosis and Management of Iron Deficiency Anemia in the 21st Century." *Therap Adv Gastroenterol*, 2011, Vol. 4, no. 3, pp. 177-84, doi:10.1177/1756283X11398736, Abstract.

Laliberte, M. "13 Ways to Deal with Menstrual Insomnia: Tossing and Turning Before your Period? You're Not Alone." 23 Jan. 2017. *Reader's Digest*, www.rd.com/health/wellness/menstrual-insomnia.

Liumbruno, G., Bennardello F., et al. "Recommendations for the Transfusion of Red Blood Cells." *Blood Transfus*, 2009, Vol. 7, no. 1, pp. 49-64, doi:10.2450/2008.0020-08.

Long, WN. "Pelvic Examination." In: Walker, HK., Hall, WD., Hurst, JW., editors. Clinical Methods: The History, Physical, and Laboratory Examinations. 3rd edition. Chap. 177, Boston: Butterworths, 1990, www.ncbi.nlm.nih.gov/books/NBK286/, Abstract.

Luckstein, K. "Exploring Treatment Options for Women with Fibroids." *Mayo Clinic*, 23 Apr. 2015, www.newsnetwork.mayoclinic.org/discussion/exploring-treatment-options-for-women-with-fibroids/.

Malik, MF., Adekola, H., et al. "Passage of Decidual Cast Following Poor Compliance with Oral Contraceptive Pill." *Fetal and Pediatric Pathology,* 2015, Vol. 34, no. 2, pp. 103-107, doi.org/10.3109/15513815.2014.970263, Abstract.

McClintock, MK. "Menstrual Synchrony and Suppression." *Nature*, 22 Jan. 1971, Vol. 229, no 5282, pp. 244-245, www.dx.doi.org/10.1038/229244a0.

McWilliams, MM. and Chennathukuzhi, VM. “Recent Advances in Uterine Fibroid Etiology.” *Semin Reprod Med*, 9 Mar. 2017, Vol. 35, no. 2, pp. 181-189, doi:10.1055/s-0037-1599090, Abstract.

“Menorrhagia.” Johns Hopkins Medicine. *Health Library*, www.hopkinsmedicine.org/healthlibrary/conditions/gynecological_health/menorrhagia_85,P00571.

“Menorrhagia (Heavy Menstrual Bleeding).” Women’s Health Network. 2018. www.womenshealthnetwork.com/pms-and-menstruation/menorrhagia.aspx.
Minkin, MJ. and Wright, CV. “A Woman's Guide to Menopause & Perimenopause.” p. 30. Yale University Press, 2005.

Minkin, MJ. and Wright, CV. “The Yale Guide to Women’s Reproductive Health: From Menarche to Menopause.” pp. 195-198. The Yale University Press, 2008.

Moreno, MA., Zuckerman AL., et al. “Premenstrual Syndrome.” *Medscape*, 1 Sep. 2016, www.emedicine.medscape.com/article/953696-overview.

“Morphine (Injection Route).” Mayo Foundation for Medical Education and Research. 1 Oct. 2018. *Mayo Clinic*, www.mayoclinic.org/drugs-supplelments/morphine-injection-route/description/drg-20074202.

Mushref, MA. and Srinivasan, S. “Effect of High Fat-Diet and Obesity on Gastrointestinal Motility.” *Ann Transl Med,* 2013, Vol. 1, no. 2, p. 14, doi:10.3978/j.issn.2305-5839.2012.11.01, Abstract.

Nagata, C., Hirokawa, K., et al. “Associations of Menstrual Pain with Intakes of Soy, Fat and Dietary Fiber in Japanese Women.” *Eur J Clin Nutr*. Jan. 2005, Vol. 59, no. 1, pp. 88-92, doi.org/10.1038/sj.ejcn.1602042, Abstract.

Nall, R. "What to Know About Vaginal Steaming." Reviewed by Ernst, H., 1 Aug. 2018, MedicalNewsToday, www.medicalnewstoday.com/articles/322657.php.

"Niacin." U.S. National Library of Medicine, 27 Jul. 2018. *MedlinePlus*, www.medlineplus.gov/druginfo/natural/924.html.

"Omega-3 Fatty Acids: An Essential Contribution." Harvard T.H. Chan School of Public Health, 2018, www.hsph.harvard.edu/nutritionsource/what-should-you-eat/fats-and-cholesterol/types-of-fat/omega-3-fats/.

"Painful Intercourse (Dyspareunia)." 12 Jan. 2018. Mayo Clinic, www.mayoclinic.org/diseases-conditions/painful-intercourse/symptoms-causes/syc-20375967.

"Pantothenic Acid." U.S. National Library of Medicine, 17 Sep. 2018. *MedlinePlus*, www.medlineplus.gov/druginfo/natural/853.html.

Parker, WH. "What Size are My Fibroids?" 4 Apr. 2013. Fibroids: A Gynecologist's Second Opinion. www.fibroidsecondopinion.com/2013/04/what-size-are-my-fibroids/.

Peddada, SD., Laughlin, SK., et al. "Growth of Uterine Leiomyomata Among Premenopausal Black and White Women." *PNAS,* 16 Dec. 2008, Vol. 105, no. 50, pp. 19887-19892, doi:10.1073/pnas.0808188105, Abstract.

"Pelvic Ultrasound." Johns Hopkins Medicine. *Health Library*, www.hopkinsmedicine.org/healthlibrary/test_procedures/gynecology/pelvic_ultrasound_92,p07784.

Pingili, R. and Jackson, W. "Decidual Cast." *The Internet Journal of Gynecology and Obstetrics*, 2007, Vol. 9, no.1, www.ispub.com/IJGO/9/1/11420, Abstract.

"Premenstrual Syndrome (PMS) and Premenstrual Dysphoric Disorder (PMDD)." 31 Aug. 2018. Center for *Young Women's Health*, www.youngwomenshealth.org/2013/10/31/pms/#.

"Pyridoxine." U.S. National Library of Medicine, 22 Oct. 2018. *MedlinePlus*, www.medlineplus.gov/druginfo/meds/a682587.html.

Rabinerson, D., Kaplan B., et al. "Membranous Dysmenorrhea: The Forgotten Entity." *Obstet Gynecol*, May 1995, Vol. 85, no. 5 Pt 2, pp. 891-892, www.doi.org/10.1016/0029-7844(94)00302-T, Abstract.

"Rapid Assessment: A Flowchart Guide to Evaluating Signs and Symptoms." p. 390, Lippincott Williams & Wilkins, 2004.

Reed, BG and Carr, BR. "The Normal Menstrual Cycle and the Control of Ovulation." 5 Aug. 2018. In: De Groot, LJ., Chrousos, G, Dungan K, et al., editors. Endotext [Internet]. South Dartmouth (MA): MDText.com, Inc.; 2000-.
www.ncbi.nlm.nih.gov/books/NBK279054, Abstract.

"Riboflavin." U.S. National Library of Medicine, 1 Oct. 2018. *MedlinePlus*, www.medlineplus.gov/ency/article/002411.htm.

Robinson N., Lorenc, A., et al. "The Evidence for Shiatsu: A Systemic Review of Shiatsu and Acupressure." *BMC Complement Altern Med*, 7 Oct. 2011, Vol. 11, no. 88, doi:10.1186/1472-6882-11-88, Abstract.

"S-Adenosyl-L-Methionine (SAMe): In Depth." National Center for Complementary and Integrative Health. Jan. 2017. *National Institutes of Health*,
www.nccih.nih.gov/health/supplements/SAMe.

"Selective Serotonin Reuptake Inhibitors (SSRIs)." 17 May 2018. *Mayo Clinic*, www.mayoclinic.org/diseases-conditions/depression/in-depth/ssris/art-20044825.

"Sex Hormone–Sensitive Gene Complex Linked to Premenstrual Mood Disorder." National Institute of Mental Health. 3 Jan. 2017. *National Institutes of Health*, www.nimh.nih.gov/news/science-news/2017/sex-hormone-sensitive-gene-complex-linked-to-premenstrual-mood-disorder.shtml, Press Release.

Silvers, WS. "Exercise-induced Allergies: The Role of Histamine Release." *Ann Allergy*, Jan. 1992, Vol. 68, no. 1, pp. 58-63, *PubMed.gov*, www.ncbi.nlm.nih.gov/pubmed/?term=Silvers%20WS%5BAuthor%5D&cauthor=true&cauthor_uid=1371041, Abstract.

"Slideshow: A Visual Guide to Uterine Fibroids." 24 May 2018. Reviewed by Todd N., *WebMD*, www.webmd.com/women/uterine-fibroids/ss/slideshow-fibroid-overview.

"St. John's Wort." 2018. *WebMD*, www.webmd.com/vitamins/ai/ingredientmono-329/st-johns-wort.

"Tai Chi and Qi Gong: In Depth." National Center for Complementary and Integrative Health, www.nccih.nih.gov/health/taichi/introduction.htm#hed1.

"Thiamin." U.S. National Library of Medicine, 1 Oct. 2018. *MedlinePlus*, www.medlineplus.gov/ency/article/002401.htm.

"Treating Premenstrual Dysphoric Disorder." Harvard Health Publications. Oct. 2009. *Harvard Medical School*, www.health.harvard.edu/womens-health/treating-premenstrual-dysphoric-disorder.

Tsibris, JCM., Segars, J., et al. "Insights from Gene Arrays on the Development and Growth Regulation of Uterine Leiomyomata." *Fertility and Sterility*, 2002, Vol. 78, no. 1, pp. 114-121, doi.org/10.1016/S0015-0282(02)03191-6, Abstract.

"The Urinary Tract & How It Works." National Institute of Diabetes and Digestive and Kidney Diseases. Jan. 2014. www.niddk.nih.gov/health-information/urologic-diseases/urinary-tract-how-it-works.

"Uterine Fibroids." The Office on Women's Health. 16 Mar. 2018. Reviewed by Eisinger, S., *WomensHealth.gov*, www.womenshealth.gov/a-z-topics/uterine-fibroids.

"Uterine Fibroids: Overview." Informed Health Online [Internet]. Cologne, Germany: Institute for Quality and Efficiency in Health Care (IQWiG). 2006-. 22 Oct. 2014. Updated 16 Nov. 2017. www.ncbi.nlm.nih.gov/books/NBK279535/.

"Vitamin A." U.S. National Library of Medicine, 2 Apr. 2015. *MedlinePlus*, www.medlineplus.gov/vitamina.html.

"Vitamin B12." U.S. National Library of Medicine, 1 Oct. 2018. *MedlinePlus*, www.medlineplus.gov/ency/article/002403.htm.

"Vitamin C." U.S. National Library of Medicine, 2 Apr. 2015. *MedlinePlus*, www.medlineplus.gov/vitaminc.html.

"Vitamin D." U.S. National Library of Medicine, 26 Mar. 2015. *MedlinePlus*, www.medlineplus.gov/vitamind.html.

"Vitamin E." U.S. National Library of Medicine, 2 Apr. 2015. *MedlinePlus*, www.medlineplus.gov/vitamine.html.

"Vitamin K." U.S. National Library of Medicine, 2 Apr. 2015. *MedlinePlus*, www.medlineplus.gov/vitamink.html.

Wang, HL. "Tofu and Tempeh as Potential Protein Sources in the Western Diet." *JAOCS*, 1984, Vol. 61, pp. 528-534. *Wiley Online Library*, www.onlinelibrary.wiley.com/doi/abs/10.1007/BF02677023, Abstract.

"What is Computed Tomography?" 23 Apr. 2014. U.S. Department of Health and Human Services. *U.S. Food and Drug Administration*, www.fda.gov/RadiationEmittingProducts/RadiationEmittingProductsandProcedures/MedicalImaging/MedicalX-Rays/ucm115318.htm.

"What to Do About Fibroids." Harvard Women's Health Watch. Jul. 2008. Harvard Health Publishing. Harvard Medical School, www.health.harvard.edu/womens-health/what_to_do_about_fibroids.

Wu, H-H. and Wang, L. "Gunner Goggles Obstetrics and Gynecology." p. 73. Elsevier, 2018.

Yang, H., Zhou, B., et al. "Proteomic Analysis of Menstrual Blood." *Molecular & cellular proteomics*, 2012, Vol. 11, no. 10, pp. 1024-1035, doi.org/10.1074/mcp.M112.018390, Abstract.

Yang, M., Feng, Y., et al. "Effectiveness of Chinese Massage Therapy (Tui Na) for Chronic Low Back Pain: Study Protocol for a Randomized Controlled Trial." *Trials*, 29 Oct. 2014, Vol. 15, no. 418, doi:10.1186/1745-6215-15-418, Abstract.

"Yarrow." Natural Medicines Comprehensive Database Consumer Version. Therapeutic Research Faculty, 2018, *WebMD*, www.webmd.com/vitamins/ai/ingredientmono-151/yarrow.